COMPOSITION OF THE ESSAY

PE
1471
.H9

 ADDISON-WESLEY PUBLISHING COMPANY
Palo Alto · Reading, Massachusetts · London · Don Mills, Ontario

COMPOSITION OF THE ESSAY

Simeon Hyde, Jr. / William H. Brown

28008

Acknowledgments

For permission to reprint copyrighted material, grateful acknowledgment is made to the following sources.

GEORGE ALLEN & UNWIN LTD.: Excerpt from *Roads to Freedom* by Bertrand Russell.

THE ATLANTIC MONTHLY: Excerpt from "The Bee's Knees" by Charles D. Stewart, published in *The Atlantic Monthly*, July, 1925.

THE CHRISTIAN CENTURY FOUNDATION: "Down to the Sea" by Theodore A. Gill, copyright 1956 Christian Century Foundation, reprinted by permission from the January 4, 1956 issue of *The Christian Century*.

THE CHRISTIAN SCIENCE MONITOR: "Anguish Too Homespun" by Henrietta Buckmaster, reprinted by permission from *The Christian Science Monitor*, © 1965 The Christian Science Publishing Society, all rights reserved.

COLLINS-KNOWLTON-WING, INC.: "The Poetry of Circumstance," by Kenneth Payson Kempton, reprinted by permission of Collins-Knowlton-Wing, Inc., copyright © 1939 by Saturday Review, Inc.

MAUDE V. CURTISS: "This Early-Bird Nonsense" by Philip Curtiss, first published in *Harper's Magazine*, January, 1933.

Dodd, Mead & Company: "The Magic Ring," reprinted by permission of Dodd, Mead & Company from *Dream Days* by Kenneth Grahame; also by permission of The Bodley Head Ltd.

R. W. Gerard: Excerpt from "Your Brain and Your Behavior" by R. W. Gerard, first published in the series "Adventures of the Mind," *Saturday Evening Post*, May 30, 1959.

Harcourt, Brace & World, Inc.: "Peculiarsome Abe," from *Abraham Lincoln: The Prairie Years*, Volume I, by Carl Sandburg, copyright 1926 by Harcourt, Brace & World, Inc.; renewed, 1954, by Carl Sandburg and reprinted by permission of the publishers.

Harper & Row Publishers, Incorporated: From *One Man's Meat* by E. B. White: "Book Learning" (July, 1942), copyright 1942 by E. B. White; excerpt from "Progress and Change" (December, 1938), copyright 1938 by E. B. White; reprinted with the permission of Harper & Row, Publishers. For use of the name Mark Twain, which is a registered trademark: "The Boy's Ambition," "I Want to be a Cub-Pilot," "A Cub-Pilot's Experience," and "A Daring Deed," from *Life on the Mississippi* by Mark Twain.

Granville Hicks: "Children, Parents, and Pirates" by Granville Hicks, first published in *Saturday Review*, June 19, 1965.

Paul B. Kinney: "The Ways of a Bear" by Paul B. Kinney, first published in *Nature Magazine*, December, 1940.

Hal Lehrman: "Where the Grass Is Always Wet" by Hal Lehrman, first published in *Saturday Review*, January 2, 1965.

Methuen & Company Ltd. Publishers: "The Mowing of a Field" from *Hills and the Sea* by Hilaire Belloc.

William Morris Agency, Inc.: "4100 Miles on a Raft" by James A. Michener, copyright © 1950 by James A. Michener, reprinted by permission of William Morris Agency, Inc., first published in *Saturday Review*, September 23, 1950.

Sheed & Ward Inc., Publishers: "On Running After One's Hat," from *All Things Considered* by G. K. Chesterton, copyright 1908, published by Sheed and Ward Inc., New York; with the kind permission of Miss Dorothy Collins and the publishers; also with the permission of Messrs. Methuen & Company Ltd.

The Society of Authors: "The Master" from *London River* by H. M. Tomlinson, reprinted with the permission of The Society of Authors as the literary representatives of the estate of H. M. Tomlinson.

Sir George Thomson: Excerpt from "What You Should Know About Physics" by Sir George Thomson, first published in the series "Adventures of the Mind," *Saturday Evening Post*, April 4, 1959.

Helen Thurber: "The Owl Who Was God," copyright © 1939 by James Thurber, from *Fables for Our Time*, published by Harper and Brothers.

Time, Inc.: The selection from "People" in *Time*, May 19, 1961.

The authors

SIMEON HYDE, JR. holds degrees from Princeton University (B.A.) and Harvard University (M.A.). He has taught English at Phillips Academy, Andover, Massachusetts, since 1950.

WILLIAM H. BROWN has taught English at Phillips Academy, Andover, Massachusetts, since 1938. He became Chairman of the Department of English in 1964. He holds degrees from Harvard University (B.A.) and Middlebury College (M.A.).

On the use of this book

The essay is a means of clarifying and communicating experience, information, and thought. In one or another of its varieties, it is the prose form which students are most frequently called upon to write, and the various structures and techniques that it employs are the basis of most of the writing that they will do in college, in business, or in professional life.

Composition of the Essay is based on the conviction that writing is best learned through close study of the practices of effective writers. The book presents a wide selection of essays grouped according to the authors' purposes and accompanied by commentaries which either point out or ask the student to point out some of the characteristics or techniques of each

essay. In all but the last section, each essay is followed by a composition assignment. These assignments usually ask the student to write an essay which has a purpose similar to that of the preceding selection and which uses some of its techniques.

The commentaries which accompany the readings require the student to develop a knowledge of terms and concepts useful in the discussion of writing. Upon first appearance these terms have been printed in boldface and defined fully enough to be understandable in context. Also printed in boldface are words from the general vocabulary which have particular application to writing. Students are expected to understand these words through the use of a dictionary.

Contents

KINDS OF WRITING

1 | *Kinds of Writing*

Although we seldom write or see isolated paragraphs, the excerpts in this section are limited to the single paragraph in order to clarify the separate characteristics of narration, description, and exposition. Later sections develop these concepts more fully through examination of the relationship of the paragraph to the essay as a whole.

From "People"

Time Magazine

"I run this place to make money, not to serve tramps," thundered Mrs. John T. Reges at the trio of drenched, mud-spattered hikers who led a march to her Old Anglers Inn near the Potomac last week and began unwrapping their home-made sandwiches. Singling out the mild-looking, silver-haired elder of the group, she barked: "Get off that rug! Get over there with the rest of the wet ones." When someone protested, she pointed at the puddles on the floor and demanded: "Well, is he going to clean up the mess?" Then she turned on the grinning youngster of the group and exploded: "You look like a bum! Get out!" He did. So did the others. When the innkeeper learned that she had just given the heave-ho to Supreme Court Justice William O. Douglas, Senator Paul H. Douglas, and Interior Secretary Stewart L. Udall, she shrugged: "I'm not even sure if I care."

COMPOSITION ASSIGNMENT

In the paragraphs from *Time*, statements and actions are recorded in the order in which they happened in time—in other words, **chronologically**. The chronological method is commonly used in the development of paragraphs of narrative writing. The use of "then" and "when" as linking words reflects the chronological development.

Write a narrative paragraph, using a chronological method of development. Be sure to choose an event that is brief enough to be reported fully in one paragraph. Try to suggest a general idea in the narrative; do not settle for a mere listing of statements and actions.

This account of an incident is an example of **narration.** Something has happened, and a reporter has recorded it. Why did he think it was worth recording? The most obvious reason is that the incident involved people of prominence: a Supreme Court justice, a United States senator, and a member of the cabinet. Much of the impact lies in the irony of the harsh and inconsiderate treatment the trio received. The reporter has enhanced this appeal by keeping their identity for the end of the paragraph. If we knew at the beginning that Mrs. Reges was thundering at Justice Douglas, Senator Douglas, and Secretary Udall, the effect of the paragraph would be lost.

Further interest lies in the fact that inns, especially those with romantic names such as Old Anglers Inn, are traditionally supposed to provide comfort and rest. Mrs. Reges violently denies the tradition and asserts at the outset that she runs "this place to make money."

Since both of these situations are based upon the contract between the behavior of the innkeeper and what we think that behavior ought to be, there is no reason that they should not be developed in the same paragraph. This is especially true since neither is explicitly stated in any one sentence, but both are implied by the paragraph as a whole.

Sentence 1 states Mrs. Reges's attitude and the situation which has caused it. It introduces but does not identify the trio. In sentence 2 Mrs. Reges concentrates her wrath on one of the group, and in sentence 3 she returns to the general attack. The last sentence identifies the trio.

Note the verbs the reporter uses to introduce Mrs. Reges's statements.

What do they have in common? How do they differ? What do they add to the narrative?

From The Private Papers of Henry Ryecroft

George Gissing

I have often heard it said that the touring cyclist has caused the revival of wayside inns. It may be so, but the touring cyclist seems to be very easily satisfied. Unless we are greatly deceived by the old writers, an English inn used to be a delightful resort, abounding in comfort, and supplied with the best of food; a place, too, where one was sure of welcome at once hearty and courteous. The inns of today, in country towns and villages, are not in that good old sense inns at all; they are merely public-houses. The landlord's chief interest is the sale of liquor. Under his roof you may, if you choose, eat and sleep, but what you are expected to do is to drink. Yet, even for drinking, there is no decent accommodation. You will find what is called a bar-parlor, a stuffy and dirty room, with crazy chairs, where only the sodden dram-gulper could imagine himself at ease. Should you wish to write a letter, only the worst pen and vilest ink is forthcoming; this even in the "commercial room" of many an inn which seems to depend upon the custom of traveling tradesmen. Indeed, this whole business of innkeeping is incredibly mismanaged. Most of all does the common ineptitude or brutality enrage one when it has possession of an old and picturesque house, such as reminds you of the best tradition, a house which might be made as comfortable as a house can be, a place of rest and mirth.

The first selection, which also had as its subject inns and inn-keeping, made no explicit statement of its point. It did suggest, however, an idea similar to the one clearly stated in this paragraph.

(a) *What is the main idea, or* **topic,** *of this paragraph?*
(b) *What is the function of each sentence in relation to the topic idea?*
(c) *Which is the* **topic sentence,** *the one which comes closest to stating the main idea?*
(d) *What principle of organization determines the order of the sentences?*

Basically, the method of this paragraph is to support an idea by presenting various circumstances which will make the idea acceptable to the reader. It is, in other words, attempting to explain and convince; it is **exposition** rather than narration.

COMPOSITION ASSIGNMENT

Write two paragraphs which center on the same idea. In the first suggest the idea through narrative. In the second state the idea and illustrate it by a set of circumstances. For a suitable topic consider your reactions to classes, sports, or other activities in which you react to the way people do things.

From The Jesuits in North America

Francis Parkman

Such was his initiation into Indian winter life. Passing over numerous adventures by water and land, we find the party, on the twelfth of November, leaving their canoes on an island, and wading ashore at low tide over the flats to the southern bank of the St. Lawrence. As two other bands had joined them, their number was increased to forty-five persons. Now, leaving the river behind, they entered those savage highlands whence issue the springs of the St. John— a wilderness of rugged mountain ranges, clad in dense, continuous forests, with no human tenant but this troop of miserable rovers, and here and there some kindred band, as miserable as they. Winter had set in, and already dead Nature was sheeted in funereal white. Lakes and ponds were frozen, rivulets sealed up, torrents encased with stalactites of ice; the black rocks and black trunks of the pine trees were beplastered with snow, and its heavy masses crushed the dull green boughs into the drifts beneath. The forest was silent as the grave.

Sentence 1 is **transitional,** linking this paragraph to the one which precedes it. The next two sentences continue the narrative of which this paragraph is a part. Starting with the fourth sentence, which begins with "now," the paragraph becomes **descriptive.** Parkman seeks to convey to the reader an **impression** of a scene, the usual purpose of description. The exact impression is not stated in any one sentence; certainly the point is not merely that the forest is silent. The reader **infers** it from the details which are given and the order in which they are arranged.

(a) *What dominant impression is suggested by the words the author uses to describe the scene?*
(b) *List the words which combine to create this impression.*

There are standard ways in which descriptive details may be arranged: near to far, far to near, left to right, right to left, top to bottom, bottom to top, or as they come into observation from a moving point of view. The arrangement is determined by the nature of what is being described

COMPOSITION ASSIGNMENT

Write a descriptive paragraph with a narrative introduction. Plan the order of details. In composing your paragraph, determine whether it is better with or without a topic sentence. If your final version does not contain a topic sentence, add one as a separate entry on your paper.

(such as a vista, a panorama, or a sky-scraper), by the way the author sees the thing (what appears important to him), and by the effect on the reader that the author feels a certain order will produce.

(c) *In what way are the details of the descriptive section of this paragraph arranged?*

From Character and Success

Theodore Roosevelt

All kinds of qualities go to make up character, for, emphatically, the term should include the positive no less than the negative virtues. If we say of a boy or a man, "He is of good character," we mean that he does not do a great many things that are wrong, and we also mean that he does do a great many things which imply much effort of the will and readiness to face what is disagreeable. He must not steal, he must not be intemperate, he must not be vicious in any way; he must not be mean or brutal; he must not bully the weak. In fact, he must refrain from whatever is evil. But besides refraining from evil, he must do good. He must be brave and energetic; he must be resolute and persevering. The Bible always inculcates the need of positive no less than the negative virtues, although certain people who profess to teach Christianity are apt to dwell wholly on the negative. We are bidden not merely to be harmless as doves, but also as wise as serpents. It is very much easier to carry out the former part of the order than the latter; while, on the other hand, it is of much importance for the good of mankind that our goodness should be accompanied by wisdom than that we should

This paragraph is an example of pure exposition. Its purpose is to clarify an idea which is introduced in the first sentence. In this paragraph the first sentence is the topic sentence.

(a) *What is the function of sentence 2? of sentence 3? of sentence 4?*

Sentence 5 is an excellent example of a transitional sentence, linking the two sections of the paragraph.

(b) *What is the function of sentence 6? of sentence 7?*
(c) *The paragraph is developed by contrasting—pointing out the differences between—two kinds of virtue. What is the relationship between these two beyond mere contrast?*

Roosevelt develops the reference to the Bible's teachings by making an **allusion** to a specific passage in the Bible. An allusion is a brief reference to something in literature or life with which the reader is presumably familiar.

(d) *Do you have any trouble relating "wise as serpents" to the main idea of the paragraph? What would you expect in its place?*

7

merely be harmless. If with the serpent wisdom we unite the serpent guile, terrible will be the damage we do; and if, with the best of intentions, we can only manage to deserve the epithet of "harmless," it is hardly worthwhile to have lived in the world at all.

(e) *In referring to serpents, Roosevelt naturally thinks of the traditional guile of the serpent, an allusion to what?*
(f) *Does his warning against guile destroy the unity of the paragraph? By this time you should be aware that a paragraph is a unit, a group of sentences built around one idea.*

COMPOSITION ASSIGNMENT

Write a unified expository paragraph, using the same method of paragraph development. Normally, the structure of a paragraph is determined by the topic and the writer's intentions toward it; that is, he has an idea and finds the appropriate form, or else idea and form develop together. Here you are being asked to reverse the usual procedure.

From Progress and Change
(December, 1938)

E. B. White

Another phase of life here which has lost something through refinement is the game of croquet. We used to have an old croquet set whose wooden balls, having been chewed by dogs, were no rounder than eggs. Paint had faded, wickets were askew. The course had been laid out haphazardly and eagerly by a child, and we all used to go out there on summer nights and play good-naturedly, with dogs romping on the lawn in the beautiful light, and the mosquitoes sniping at us, and everyone in good spirits, racing after balls and making split shots for the sheer love of battle. Last spring we decided that the croquet set was beyond use, and invested in a rather fancy new one with hoops set in small wooden sockets, and mallets with rubber faces. The course is now exactly seventy-two feet long and we lined the wickets

By way of a summary, we may see in the preceding selections some basic principles of paragraph composition.

There are three kinds of writing: narrative, descriptive, and expository. Narration deals with event, description with impression, and exposition with explanation, usually of an idea. Although these kinds of writing seldom are found in isolation, a piece can be classified according to its purpose. Thus, although *The Private Papers of Henry Ryecroft* contains descriptive sections, it is basically expository; and, although *The Jesuits in North America* begins as a continuation of narrative, its basic purpose is to describe.

Questions have been directed to different methods of paragraph development. The paragraph from *Time* magazine is developed chronologically; the event is reported in the order of time. The selection from *The Private Papers of Henry Ryecroft* is developed by contrasting the inns of former days with the inns of Gissing's day. In order to make clear the contrast, Gissing provides up with a string; but the little boy is less fond of it now, for we make him keep still while we are shooting. A dog isn't even allowed to cast his shadow across the line of play. There are frequent quarrels of a minor nature, and it seems to me we return from the field of honor tense and out of sorts.

COMPOSITION ASSIGNMENT

To see how well you have mastered the principles noted in the commentary, write an analysis of the selection from "Progress and Change." Do not merely restate the ideas, but answer the following questions.

(a) *What is the topic idea?*
(b) *What does each sentence contribute to the development of the topic idea?*
(c) *What method of development is used to achieve coherence?*
(d) *As what kind of writing would you classify this?*

examples of the lack of comfort and graciousness in the modern inn. The selection from *The Jesuits in North America* in its descriptive section is developed by the arrangement of detail in an order suggested by the scene described. Finally, the paragraph by Theodore Roosevelt, like Gissing's paragraph, is built on contrast and example, although the examples are not as specific as those in Gissing's. There are other methods of paragraph development which will be discussed in later sections.

It should be evident from some of the questions that a paragraph should have **unity**—that is, should be focused on one idea, impression, or event. Necessary to this unity is **coherence,** the clear and close connection of sentences within a paragraph. Coherence is gained by the method or combination of methods of paragraph development and aided by transitional words, phrases, and sometimes sentences.

NARRATIVE WRITING

2 | *Narrative Writing*

The essays in this section are all narrative. Although they do contain description and exposition, they present events which follow one another to a conclusion. Nevertheless they are not short stories, but essays in that the interest we take in them goes beyond the succession of events which is merely a vehicle for the observations on life which they contain.

THE OWL WHO WAS GOD

James Thurber

"The Owl Who Was God" is a complete short narrative in the familiar form of the beast fable. The author tells his story without expository development of its significance; that is, he does not explicitly interpret or editorialize, but leaves it to the reader to see how the story applies to human life. The reader should realize that the "moral" is not an adequate statement of the significance of the fable.

[1] Once upon a starless midnight there was an owl who sat on the branch of an oak tree. Two ground moles tried to slip quietly by, unnoticed. "You!" said the owl. "Who?" they quavered, in fear and astonishment, for they could not believe it was possible for anyone to see them in that thick darkness. "You two!" said the owl. The moles hurried away and told the other creatures of the field and forest that the owl was the greatest and wisest of all animals because he could answer any question. "I'll see about that," said a secretary bird, and he called on the owl one night when it was again very dark. "How many claws am I holding up?" said the secretary bird. "Two," said the owl, and that was right. "Can you give me another expression for 'that is to say' or 'namely'?" asked the secretary bird. "To wit," said the owl. "Why does a lover call on his love?" asked the secretary bird. "To woo," said the owl.

[2] The secretary bird hastened back to the other creatures and reported that the owl was

[1] Note that the first sentence uses a variation of the time-honored formula for introducing a story.

(a) *What is the formula?*

Thurber's variation shows the humor that often results from the substitution of a **concrete** for an **abstract** term.

There are no strict rules for paragraphing narrative, but where there is a change of scene, or a new stage in the development of the action, or a shift in focus, it is usually best to begin a new paragraph. In this paragraph there are two stages of action and a shift of focus from the moles to the secretary bird. Yet the paragraph has unity.

(b) *With what is the paragraph entirely concerned?*

indeed the greatest and wisest animal in the world because he could see in the dark and because he could answer any question. "Can he see in the daytime, too?" asked a red fox. "Yes," echoed a dormouse and a French poodle. "Can he see in the daytime, too?" All the other creatures laughed loudly at this silly question, and they set upon the red fox and his friends and drove them out of the region. Then they sent a messenger to the owl and asked him to be their leader.

☐3 When the owl appeared among the animals it was high noon and the sun was shining brightly. He walked very slowly, which gave him an appearance of great dignity, and he peered about him with large, staring eyes, which gave him an air of tremendous importance. "He's God!" screamed a Plymouth Rock hen. And the others took up the cry "He's God!" So they followed him wherever he went and when he began to bump into things they began to bump into things, too. Finally he came to a concrete highway and he started up the middle of it and all the other creatures followed him. Presently a hawk, who was acting as outrider, observed a truck coming towards them at fifty miles an hour, and he reported to the secretary bird and the secretary bird reported to the owl. "There's danger ahead," said the secretary bird. "To wit?" said the owl. The secretary bird told him. "Aren't you afraid?" he asked. "Who?" said the owl calmly, for he could not see the truck. "He's God!" cried all the creatures again, and they were still crying "He's God!" when the truck hit them and ran them down. Some of the animals were merely injured, but most of them, including the owl, were killed.

Moral: You can fool too many of the people too much of the time.

☐2 This paragraph continues to describe the actions of the secretary bird.

(a) *What accounts for the author's use of a new paragraph?*
(b) *What is the point of the other animals' treatment of the red fox and his friends?*
(c) *Have the characteristics of particular animals led the author to choose them for particular roles?*

☐3 Consider the behavior of the hen and her followers.

(a) *What is represented by the behavior of these animals?*
(b) *Why is the hen an appropriate choice to utter these particular words of judgment about the owl?*
(c) *What is the point of the way the hawk's report is passed on to the owl?*

Notice the focus of the last sentence. The emphasis is on the animals in general; the owl is mentioned in a subordinate phrase.

(d) *How does the focus of the last sentence reflect and emphasize the major focus or chief concern of the tale?*

The Moral is a variation of Abraham Lincoln's familiar maxim.

(a) *What is the original?*
(b) *Which moral is the more pessimistic observation?*

SUMMARY

"The Owl Who Was God" does not reflect or create an interest in animals as such. It is a comment on the behavior of human beings, through the device of placing them in the guise of animals. Since it ridicules human folly, it is an example of **satire.**

COMPOSITION ASSIGNMENT

Write a beast fable; to do so, tell the story of an event involving two or more animals but representing relations among men. Try to choose animals that have, or are traditionally supposed to have, characteristics which suggest human qualities. You may, but need not, attach a moral as Thurber has done.

ESSEX IN IRELAND

James Anthony Froude

Even in fiction, we seldom find pure narrative, for the author usually intends to present, not a mere sequence of events, but his interpretation or judgment of those events. In this excerpt, narrative, descriptive, and expository paragraphs are combined to give the writer's interpretation of an historical event.

[1] The work of the expedition, however, was not over. It had yet to receive its crowning distinction. Ulster, as Essex* admitted, was quiet; but, quiet or not quiet, wolves were still wolves, to be exterminated wherever they could be caught.

---

* *Essex:* the Earl of Essex, a favorite of Queen Elizabeth of England. Charged by her with the conquest of Ireland, he massacred Irish lords and Scots lords who held lands in Ireland. The time is the end of the sixteenth century.

[1] This short paragraph is an expository introduction; the author uses it to suggest an interpretation of the episode he is about to narrate.

(a) *At first reading, what seems to be Froude's attitude toward the story he is introducing?*
(b) *What phrase seems to convey an explicit judgment on the coming episode?*

In his comment about "wolves," Froude is actually referring to people. Thus, his use of the word is not **literal,** but **figurative.**

(c) *Does "extermination of wolves" support the author's apparent judgment of the episode or does it imply a different sort of judgment?*

2 On the coast of Antrim, not far from the Giant's Causeway, lies the singular Island of Rathlin. It is formed of basaltic rock, encircled with precipices, and is accessible only at a single spot. It contains an area of about four thousand acres, of which a thousand are sheltered and capable of cultivation, the rest being heather and rock. The approach is at all times dangerous; the tide sets fiercely through the strait which divides the island from the mainland, and when the wind is from the west, the Atlantic swell renders it impossible to land. The situation and difficulty of access had thus long marked Rathlin as a place of refuge for Scotch or Irish fugitives, and besides its natural strength it was respected as a sanctuary, having been the abode at one time of Saint Columba.* A mass of broken masonry on a cliff overhanging the sea is a remnant of the castle in which Robert Bruce† watched the leap of the legendary spider. To this island, when Essex entered Antrim, Macconnell and the other Scots had sent their wives and children, their aged and their sick, for safety.

3 On his way through Carrickfergus, when returning to Dublin, the Earl ascertained that they had not yet been brought back to their homes. The officer in command of the English garrison (it is painful to mention the name either of him or of any man concerned with what ensued) was John Norris, Lord Norris's second son, so famous afterwards in the Low

---

* *Saint Columba* (Latin *dove*): an Irish missionary who Christianized northern Scotland and became head of the Church in Scotland.

---

† *Robert Bruce:* King of Scotland. Inspired by the successful leap of the spider, he returned from exile on Rathlin to regain control of his realm.

2 This paragraph is descriptive. Note the order in which the details are presented. The first sentence gives us the location of the island; the second, its general topography with emphasis on a feature important to the story; the third, an estimate of its size and a general impression of the terrain. The fourth picks up the significant idea of the second, emphasizing the difficulty of invasion. Sentence 5 is important to the coherence of the paragraph because the phrase "situation and difficulty of access" summarizes the foregoing details and leads into the idea of refuge and sanctuary, which proves to be the topic idea of the paragraph. The phrase is thus a transitional phrase. Because the sentence in which it occurs expresses the topic idea, it is the topic sentence. (Note that the first sentence merely introduces; it does not express the topic idea.)

How do the allusions to persons of some importance in history or legend contribute to the topic idea of the paragraph and to the main idea, or **theme,** *of the selection?*

When you have read the entire excerpt, you should be able to explain the importance of this paragraph in determining the reader's response to the story that follows it.

3 This paragraph returns the reader to Froude's story of the events of Essex's expedition. It is narrative, an account of the actions on the island.

(a) *How does the statement in parentheses relate to the judgment suggested in the first paragraph?*

Countries, grandson of Sir Henry Norris executed for adultery with Anne Boleyn. Three small frigates were in the harbor. The summer had been dry, hot, and windless. The sea was smooth; there was a light and favorable air from the east; and Essex directed Norris to take a company of soldiers with him, cross over and kill whatever he could find. The run up the Antrim coast was rapidly and quietly accomplished. Before an alarm could be given the English had landed, close to the ruins of the church which bears Saint Columba's name. Bruce's castle was then standing, and was occupied by a score or two of Scots, who were in charge of the women. But Norris had brought cannon with him. The weak defenses were speedily destroyed and after a fierce assault, in which several of the garrison were killed, the chief who was in command offered to surrender, if he and his people were allowed to return to Scotland. The conditions were rejected; the Scots yielded, and every living creature in the place except the chief and his family, who were probably reserved for ransom, was immediately put to the sword. Two hundred were killed in the castle. It was then discovered that several hundred more, chiefly mothers and their little ones, were hidden in the caves about the shore. There was no remorse, not even the faintest shadow of perception that the occasion called for it. They were hunted out as if they had been seals or otters, and all destroyed. Surleyboy* and the other chiefs, Essex coolly wrote, had sent their wives and children into the island, "which be all taken and executed to the number of six hundred." Surleyboy himself, he continued, "stood upon the mainland of the Glynnes and saw the taking of the island, and

After explaining who the officer in command of the Dublin garrison was, Froude describes the harbor and the weather conditions.

(b) *How are these descriptive details given point by the preceding paragraph?*
(c) *What is the purpose of again mentioning St. Columba and Bruce?*
(d) *What other details acquire significance or emphasis from the preceding paragraph?*
(e) *How are the references to mothers and little ones hidden in caves and to seals and otters related to the introductory paragraphs?*
(f) *What is the effect of "coolly wrote"?*

---

* Surleyboy: Sarle boigh Macconnell. The name means Sarley, or Charley, the yellow-haired.

was likely to have run mad for sorrow, tearing and tormenting himself, and saying that he there lost all that he ever had."

④ The impression left upon the mind by this horrible story is increased by the composure with which even the news of it was received. "Yellow-haired Charley" might tear himself for "his pretty littles and their dam," but in Ireland itself the massacre was not specially distinguished in the general system of atrocity. Essex described it himself as one of the exploits with which he was most satisfied, and Elizabeth in answer to his letters bade him tell John Norris, "the executioner of his well designed enterprise, that she would not be unmindful of his services." But though passed over and unheeded at the time, and lying buried for three hundred years, the bloody stain comes back to light again, not in myth and legend, but in the original account of the nobleman by whose command the deed was done, and when the history of England's dealings with Ireland settles at last into its final shape, that hunt among the caves of Rathlin will not be forgotten. It is some satisfaction to learn that an officer and forty of the soldiers, who had been concerned in it, were cut off three months after, near Carrickfergus. Essex himself went back in the autumn to England, to gather together what remained of his property and arrange for the payment of his debts.

④ The last paragraph is expository. Here the author directly sets forth his judgment of the massacre. Compare "horrible story" with "crowning distinction" in the first paragraph. Before they reach this point, attentive readers will have realized that various details along the way contradict the judgment stated in the introductory paragraph. Clearly the author has meant the reader to discover that he means the opposite of what he says in paragraph 1. The device is called **verbal irony,** irony of statement.

The paragraph is carefully developed. Observe how the author has caused those responsible for the deed to condemn themselves in our eyes. The guilt falls on Elizabeth as well as on her officers.

In Froude's view, does it end there?

COMPOSITION ASSIGNMENT

Write an account of an action carried out by a person or group of persons. You should follow Froude's scheme of organization, which consists of setting forth circumstances and scene (description), presenting a sequence of events (narration), and finally expressing interpretation and judgment (exposition). You may be able to use some of the devices that he uses to maintain coherence and communicate his interpretation along the way. A suggestion (which should apply to your writing in general) is that you write of persons and events that you know at first hand—the consequences of a thoughtless prank or the outcome of some community project rather than a massacre or military victory.

THE MASTER

H. M. Tomlinson

[1] This master of a ship I remember first as a slim lad, with a shy smile, and large hands that were lonely beyond his outgrown reefer jacket. His cap was always too small for him, and the soiled frontal badge of his line became a colored button beyond his forelock. He used to come home occasionally—and it was always when we were on the point of forgetting him altogether. He came with a huge bolster in a cab, as though out of the past and nowhere. There is a tradition, a book tradition, that the boy apprenticed to the sea acquires saucy eyes, and a self-reliance always ready to dare to that bleak extreme the very thought of which horrifies those who are lawful and cautious. They know better who live where the ships are. He used to bring his young shipmates to see us, and they were like himself. Their eyes were

For each of the paragraphs of this selection—except the first, for which an example is provided—you will be asked to copy down the topic sentence if one exists or to compose a summary sentence which might serve as a topic sentence.

[1] The first four sentences describe a young man by presenting various details that should suggest particular characteristics. No generalizing adjectives are used.

(a) *What adjectives might be used to characterize the young man in general terms?*

(b) *What advantages does the author's combination of specific details have over a general characterization?*

Frequently, a paragraph achieves unity by developing a clear relationship between several subjects. Sentence 5 abruptly shifts from the "lad" to a description of the traditional image of the young sailor.

(c) *In what respects does this description contrast with that of the lad?*

downcast. They showed no self-reliance. Their shyness and politeness, when the occasion was quite simple, were absurdly incommensurate even with modesty. Their sisters, not nearly so polite, used to mock them.

2 As our own shy lad was never with us for long, his departure being as abrupt and unannounced as his appearance, we could willingly endure him. But he was extraneous to the household. He had the impeding nature of a new and superfluous piece of furniture which is in the way, yet never knows it, and placidly stays where it is, in its wooden manner, till it is placed elsewhere. There was a morning when, as he was leaving the house, during one of his brief visits to his home, I noticed to my astonishment that he had grown taller than myself. How had that happened? And where? I had followed him to the door that morning because, looking down at his cap which he was nervously handling, he had told me he was going then to an examination. About a week later he announced, in a casual way, that he had got his master's ticket. After the first shock of surprise, caused by the fact that this information was an unexpected warning of our advance in years, we were amused, and we congratulated him. Naturally he had got his certificate as master mariner. Why not? Nearly all the mates we knew got it, sooner or later. That was bound to come. But very soon after that he gave us a genuine surprise, and made us anxious. He informed us, as casually, that he had been appointed master to a ship; a very different matter from merely possessing the license to command.

3 We were even alarmed. This was serious. He could not do it. He was not the man to make a command for anything. A fellow who, not so long ago, used to walk a mile with a

After commenting on the inaccuracy of tradition, the author justifies his comment by **comparing** the lad with his shipmates—that is, pointing out similarities between them. Their common qualities contrast with the traditional image. The paragraph ends with a reference to the sisters' mockery of the young sailors. In all, four subjects are referred to—the lad, the traditional image, the shipmates, and the sisters; yet all these are introduced for the sole purpose of developing the paragraph topic by both comparison and contrast.

The topic idea can be expressed by a simple generalization: This master of a ship I remember first as a gawky, unconfident lad. This statement can be amplified to summarize the relationship between the topic idea and subordinate ideas. The resulting statement would be a summary, or **abstract,** of the paragraph:

> This master of a ship I remember first as being a gawky, unconfident lad, quite unlike the traditional image of the resolute young mariner but like his shipmates, whose shyness was mocked by their sisters.

2 Note how "our own shy lad" refocuses attention on the subject of the essay. This paragraph is a complex one. The first part tells something of the narrator's relationship with the lad; the second part records the narrator's reaction to certain events in the lad's life.

(a) *How does the first part combine with the previous paragraph to explain the narrator's shock and anxiety?*
(b) *Write a sentence that summarizes this paragraph.*

3 Note the transition. The phrase "even alarmed" clearly shows that this paragraph is a climactic development

telegram because he had not the strength of character to face the lady clerk in the post office round the corner, was hardly the man to overawe a crowd of hard characters gathered by chance from Tower Hill,* socialize them, and direct them successfully in subduing the conflicting elements of a difficult enterprise. Not he. But we said nothing to discourage him.

4 Of course, he was a delightful fellow. He often amused us, and he did not always know why. He was frank, he was gentle, but that large vacancy, the sea, where he had spent most of his young life, had made him—well, slow. You know what I mean. He was curiously innocent of those dangers of great cities which are nothing to us because we know they are there. Yet he was always on the alert for thieves and parasites. I think he enjoyed his belief in their crafty omnipresence ashore. Proud of his alert and knowing intelligence, he would relate a long story of the way he had not only frustrated an artful shark, but had enjoyed the process in perfect safety. That we, who rarely went out of London, never had such adventures, did not strike him as worth a thought or two. He never paused in his merriment to consider the strange fact that to him, alone of our household, such wayside adventures fell. With a shrewd air he would inform us that he was about to put the savings of a voyage into an advertised trap which a country parson would have stepped over without a second contemptuous glance.

5 He took his ship away. The affair was not discussed at home, though each of us gave it some private despondency. We followed him silently, apprehensively, through the reports in

---

* *Tower Hill:* an area neighboring the Tower of London and once used for state executions.

of the surprise recorded in the previous one. Note also the informal use of "this" to refer to the appointment as master mentioned at the end of the previous paragraph. The use of a pronoun which does not have a specific noun antecedent is ordinarily avoided in formal prose. However, in this case the meaning is clear and the transition effective.

(a) *Identify the topic sentence.*
(b) *Note that it is supported by an **inference** drawn from an **example**. Does the reasoning seem sound?*
(c) *The judgment that "he was not the man" reflects what **point of view**—that of the time the impression was formed or the author's view at the time of writing?*
(d) *If there is any irony, are we aware of it at this point in our reading (or only after completing the essay)?*

4 (a) *Which sentence do you think is the topic sentence? If you do not find an adequate one, compose your own summary sentence. Be prepared to defend what you have done.*

The most interesting quality of this paragraph is its **tone**—the author's control of language to suggest his attitude toward the event he is narrating. The narrator seems to be ridiculing the boy. Actually, the tone indicates that the irony is at his own expense.

(b) *Where do you find indications that the author is ridiculing his own attitude at the time?*

5 This paragraph is the beginning of a narrative sequence. Observe that, like many of the paragraphs that follow, it begins with a simple statement of action that marks a new stage in the course of events.

The brief summary of events contained in the paragraph is made significant by the statement of the

the *Shipping Gazette*. He made point after point safely—St. Vincent, Gibraltar, Suez, Aden—after him we went across to Colombo, Singapore, and at length we learned that he was safe at Batavia. He had got that steamer out all right. He got her home again, too. After his first adventure as master he made voyage after voyage with no more excitement in them than you would find in Sunday walks in a suburb. It was plain luck; or else navigation and seamanship were greatly overrated arts.

[6] A day came when he invited me to go with him part of his voyage. I could leave the ship at Bordeaux. I went. You must remember that we had never seen his ship. And there he was, walking with me to the dock from a Welsh railway station, a man in a cheap mackintosh, with an umbrella I will not describe, and he was carrying a brown paper parcel. He was appropriately crowned with a bowler hat several sizes too small for him. Glancing up at his profile, I actually wondered whether the turmoil was now going on in his mind over that confession which now he was bound to make; that he was not the master of a ship, and never had been.

[7] There she was, a bulky modern freighter, full of derricks and time-saving appliances, and her funnel lording it over the neighborhood. The man with the parcel under his arm led me up the gangway. I was not yet convinced. I was, indeed, less sure than ever that he could be the master of this huge community of engines and men. He did not accord with it.

[8] We were no sooner on deck than a man in uniform, gray-haired, with a seamed and resolute face, which anyone would have recognized at once as a sailor's, approached us. He was introduced as the chief officer. He had a tale

narrator's apprehension which introduces it and by the concluding statement, which gives alternative explanations of why his expectations were not fulfilled.

(a) *What is the point of view of the last sentence of this paragraph—a final judgment at the time of writing or a record of what the author thought at the time?*
(b) *What effect does the author intend the final statement to have?*
(c) *Write a sentence which summarizes the point of the paragraph.*

[6], [7], [8] These paragraphs introduce the climactic incident which the preceding paragraphs have prepared us for. Taken together, they have a unity which comes from the narrator's sense of an **incongruity.** Although the three paragraphs make a unit, they are treated separately because each marks a distinct stage of the action.

Write a sentence that summarizes the incongruity.

of woe: trouble with the dockmaster, with the stevedores, with the cargo, with many things. He did not appear to know what to do with them. He was asking this boy of ours.

[9] The skipper began to speak. At that moment I was gazing at the funnel, trying to decipher a monogram upon it; but I heard a new voice, rapid and incisive, sure of its subject, resolving doubts, and making the crooked straight. It was the man with the brown paper parcel. That was still under his arm—in fact, the parcel contained pink pajamas, and there was hardly enough paper. The respect of the mate was not lessened by this.

[10] The skipper went to gaze down a hatchway. He walked to the other side of the ship, and inspected something there. Conned her length, called up in a friendly but authoritative way to an engineer standing by an amidship rail above. He came back to the mate, and with an easy precision directed his will on others, through his deputy, up to the time of sailing. He beckoned to me, who also, apparently, was under his august orders, and turned, as though perfectly aware that in this place I should follow him meekly, in full obedience.

[11] Our steamer moved out at midnight, in a drive of wind and rain. There were bewildering and unrelated lights about us. Peremptory challenges were shouted to us from nowhere. Sirens blared out of dark voids. And there was the skipper on the bridge, the lad who caused us amusement at home, with this confusion in the dark about him, and an immense insentient mass moving with him at his will; and he had his hands in his pockets, and turned to tell me what a cold night it was. The pier-head searchlight showed his face, alert, serene, with his brows knitted in a little frown,

[9], [10], [11]   These paragraphs make up another unit, concerned with the narrator's enlightenment, or discovery of the true situation.

Write a sentence that states the essence of the discovery. Why is there a shift from "this boy of ours" in the last sentence of paragraph 8 to the "skipper" in the first sentence of 9?

[11]   Observe that this paragraph serves not only to complete the account of the climactic episode, but also to pull the entire essay together. The narrator might have ended the story of his voyage and then added a conclusion, a paragraph of summary and interpretation. What he has done instead is more artful and probably more agreeable because it is not so heavy-handed as a distinct conclusion might be.

(a) *Identify the first phrase that takes us back to the early part of the selection. Which paragraphs does it echo?*

and his underlip projecting as the sign of the pride of those who look direct into the eyes of an opponent, and care not at all. In my berth that night I searched for a moral for this narrative, but went to sleep before I found it.

SUMMARY

We see that the narrator has been misled. The outcome of his voyage with the master and his final judgment of him were different from what he had expected. We have here an example of another sort of irony, called **irony of outcome.** It consists of a discrepancy between expectation and outcome, or between intention and result.

Read over the topic sentences that you have selected or composed. Together, they should make an abstract, or **sentence outline,** of "The Master." The making of such an abstract, paragraph by paragraph, is an excellent way to insure comprehension of a difficult piece of reading and to learn by observation the principles of composition. Such an outline can also be an effective way to organize your own writing, for it can help you to keep clearly in mind the main theme and purpose as well as the relation of the parts to the whole. In doing so, it can help you to avoid **digression**—wandering away from the topic—or including irrelevant detail.

"The Master" is probably best classified not as a short story, but as a narrative essay. There is little **plot** in the strict sense of the word, for there is no **conflict** of crucial importance to the characters, nor suspense, excitement, or vital question of outcome. Note that at no point does the narrator step aside and cause the reader to lose himself in the action. Instead, the focus is always on the narrator's response to the behavior of the master. No paragraph is purely a narrative of action, for in each the narrator gives us his conception of the character of the master as it appeared to him at the time. Furthermore, as the analyses of paragraphs 3, 4, and 5 are intended to point out, any element of surprise is lessened by foreshadowing of the final irony. In an important sense the subject of the piece is the narrator rather

(b) *The next-to-last sentence should recall which previous paragraph?*
(c) *. What would be lost if the title were "The Skipper" or "The Shipmaster"?*

When asked to state the theme of "The Master," students are often content with the maxim, "You can't judge a book by its cover." This is probably an inadequate statement of the human significance of the narrator's misjudgment.

(d) *Consider the difference between the worlds of the seaman and the narrator and consider the attitudes of elders toward the young; then try to write a better statement of the truth that the author has recognized.*

than the master. It is true that we cannot be sure whether the events actually occurred as they are recounted here or whether the narrator is identical with the author himself, but for the reasons given, the piece can be regarded as an example of the **personal essay,** or to use an alternative term, the **familiar essay.** Both terms designate a subjective piece of writing, one in which we feel that the author's primary concern is the sharing of an attitude or discovery about life, not **didactically,** in the manner of a sermon or lecture, but informally; and frequently in such a way as to make us feel that we share with the author a common humanity.

COMPOSITION ASSIGNMENT

Write a narrative essay which is like "The Master" in that you tell of your experience in coming to know another person or of the effect another person has had upon you. The word *narrative* should be a reminder that the essay is to be built upon an event or sequence of related events.

THE MAGIC RING

Kenneth Grahame

[1] Grown-up people really ought to be more careful. Among themselves it may seem but a small thing to give their word and take back their word. For them there are so many compensations. Life lies at their feet, a party-colored india-rubber ball; they may kick it this way or kick it that, it turns up blue, yellow, or green, but always colored and glistening. Thus one sees it happen almost every day, and, with a jest and a laugh, the thing is over, and the disappointed one turns to fresh pleasure, lying ready to his hand. But with those who are below them, whose little globe is swayed by them, who rush to build star-pointing alhambras on their most casual word, they really ought to be more careful.

[2] In this case of the circus, for instance, it was not as if we had led up to the subject. It was they who began it entirely—prompted thereto by the local newspaper. "What, a circus!" said they, in their irritating, casual way: "that would be nice to take the children to. Wednesday would be a good day. Suppose we go on Wednesday. Oh, and pleats are being worn again, with rows of deep braid," etc.

[3] What the others thought I know not; what they said, if they said anything, I did not comprehend. For me the house was bursting, walls seemed to cramp and to stifle, the roof was jumping and lifting. Escape was the imperative thing—to escape into the open air, to shake off bricks and mortar, and to wander in the unfrequented places of the earth, the more properly to take in the passion and the promise of the giddy situation.

[1] The engaging informality of this essay can be appreciated immediately if Kenneth Grahame's opening is compared with the following "introduction," characteristic of the formal essay.

> An unfortunate tendency of adults is the inability to recognize that their failure to give children what they have promised them creates disappointments much keener than those suffered by adults, who can easily find a new pleasure to replace the one they have lost.

Grahame's method differs from that of the formal introduction not only in its informal tone but also in his use of particulars to suggest the idea. "Party-colored india-rubber ball" is an example of figurative language, in this instance **metaphor**—that is, an implied comparison, which introduces an image to suggest an idea.

(a) *What other terms are used metaphorically?*

Observe the repetition of the first sentence as the main clause of the last.

(b) *What is the value of the repetition?*

[2] With a simple "we" and "they" Grahame has established the point of view of the essay. (Note that here point of view is used in a sense somewhat different from, but related to, the use of the term on page 22, paragraph 3 and page 23, paragraph 5.)

(a) *How has the author engaged our sympathy with the "we" rather than the "they"?*

(b) *What is the value of the direct quotation?*

[3] The paragraph conveys the mood of the narrator without using general, or abstract, words denoting a state of mind.

[4] Nature seemed prim and staid that day and the globe gave no hint that it was flying round a circus ring of its own. Could they really be true, I wondered, all those bewildering things I had heard tell of circuses? Did long-tailed ponies really walk on their hind-legs and fire off pistols? Was it humanly possible for clowns to perform one-half of the bewitching drolleries recorded in history? And how, oh, how dare I venture to believe that, from off the backs of creamy Arab steeds, ladies of more than earthly beauty discharged themselves through paper hoops? No, it was not altogether possible, there must have been some exaggeration. Still, I would be content with very little, I would take a low percentage—a very small proportion of the circus myth would more than satisfy me. But again, even supposing that history were, once in a way, no liar, could it be that I myself was really fated to look upon this thing in the flesh and to live through it, to survive the rapture? No, it was altogether too much. Something was bound to happen, one of us would develop measles, the world would blow up with a loud explosion. I must not dare, I must not presume, to entertain the smallest hope. I must endeavor sternly to think of something else.

[5] Needless to say, I thought, I dreamed of nothing else, day or night. Waking, I walked arm-in-arm with a clown, and cracked a portentous whip to the brave music of a band. Sleeping, I pursued—perched astride of a coal-black horse—a princess all gauze and spangles, who always managed to keep just one unattainable length ahead. In the early morning Harold and I, once fully awake, cross-examined each other as to the possibilities of this or that circus tradition, and exhausted the lore long ere the first housemaid was stirring. In this state of exaltation we slipped onward to what

(a) *Using the first person point of view ("I felt . . ."), write a sentence that states explicitly how the narrator felt.*
(b) *Would the paragraph be improved by the addition of such a sentence?*

[4] Observe that this paragraph does not describe a static, or unchanging, condition, but rather narrates an evolution, or development, of a state of mind. Coherence is achieved by careful transition from one stage to the next.

(a) *Describe the development and point out the transitional words and phrases.*

Another means of holding the paragraph together and giving it a rhythmic movement is the repetition of sentence patterns, words, and phrases.

(b) *Point them out in the text.*

The paragraph is evidence that repetition, far from being always a stylistic weakness, can be a source of strength. Compare the following with Grahame's last three sentences.

> I must not dare. To presume to entertain the smallest hope would be wrong. It was necessary to endeavor sternly to think of something else.

[5] (a) *What word brings the narrator back to his "text"?*
(b) *What is the meaning of "text" in this context?*

promised to be a day of all white days—which brings me right back to my text, that grown-up people really ought to be more careful.

[6] I had known it could never really be; I had said so to myself a dozen times. The vision was too sweetly ethereal for embodiment. Yet the pang of the disillusionment was none the less keen and sickening, and the pain was as that of a corporeal wound. It seemed strange and foreboding, when we entered the breakfast room, not to find everybody cracking whips, jumping over chairs, and whooping in ecstatic rehearsal of the wild reality to come. The situation became grim and pallid indeed, when I caught the expressions "garden party" and "my mauve tulle," and realized that they both referred to that very afternoon. And every minute, as I sat silent and listened, my heart sank lower and lower, descending relentlessly like a clock weight into my bootsoles.

[7] Throughout my agony I never dreamed of resorting to a direct question, much less a reproach. Even during the period of joyful anticipation some fear of breaking the spell had kept me from any bald circus talk in the presence of them. But Harold, who was built in quite another way, so soon as he discerned the drift of their conversation and heard the knell of all his hopes, filled the room with wail and clamor of bereavement. The grinning welkin rang with "Circus!" "Circus!" shook the windowpanes; the mocking walls re-echoed "Circus!" Circus he would have, and the whole circus, and nothing but the circus. No compromise for him, no evasions, no fallacious, unsecured promises to pay. He had drawn his check on the Bank of Expectation, and it had got to be cashed then and there; else he would yell, and yell himself into a fit, and come out of it and yell again. Yelling should be his profession, his art, his mission, his career. He was

[6] Note that the narrator tells us of the effect of his disappointment before explaining how it came about.

(a) *Can you think of any reason that he does this instead of following chronological order?*

Consider the point of view.

(b) *How closely do we observe the adults?*
(c) *What is the contrast on which the effect of the paragraph depends?*
(d) *How do the quoted fragments of conversation relate to the comments of the first paragraph?*

[7] The use of a general term to summarize what has been implied or described in specific terms is an excellent and easily used means of transition.

(a) *Which word in the first sentence accomplishes the transition from the previous paragraph?*

Note the consistent development of the figurative, or metaphoric, description of Harold's yelling that begins with "unsecured promises to pay."

(b) *What other words and phrases contribute to this sustained metaphor?*

29

qualified, he was resolute, and he was in no hurry to retire from the business.

[8] The noisy ones of the world, if they do not always shout themselves into the imperial purple, are sure at least of receiving attention. If they cannot sell everything at their own price, one thing—silence—must, at any cost, be purchased of them. Harold accordingly had to be consoled by the employment of every specious fallacy and base-born trick known to those whose doom it is to handle children. For me their hollow cajolery had no interest. I could pluck no consolation out of their bankrupt though prodigal pledges. I only waited till that hateful, well-known "Some other time, dear!" told me that hope was finally dead. Then I left the room without any remark. It made it worse—if anything could—to hear that stale, worn-out old phrase, still supposed by those dullards to have some efficacy.

[9] To nature, as usual, I drifted by instinct, and there, out of the track of humanity, under a friendly hedgerow had my black hour unseen. The world was a globe no longer, space was no more filled with whirling circuses of spheres. That day the old beliefs rose up and asserted themselves, and the earth was flat again— ditch-riddled, stagnant, and deadly flat. The undeviating roads crawled straight and white, elms dressed themselves stiffly along inflexible hedges, all nature, centrifugal no longer, sprawled flatly in lines out to its farthest edge, and I felt just like walking out to that terminus, and dropping quietly off. Then, as I sat there, morosely chewing bits of stick, the recollection came back to me of certain fascinating advertisements I had spelled out in papers—advertisements of great and happy men, owning big ships of tonnage running into four figures, who

[8] Again observe that one word establishes the connection between the first sentence and the previous paragraph. Also observe in the middle of the paragraph the return to the metaphoric language of the previous paragraph.

[9] (a) *The second sentence echoes which paragraphs?*
(b) *To which of these is this paragraph more closely related?*
(c) *What is the nature of this relationship?*

Observe that the author does not discuss his state of mind, but suggests it by describing the appearance the world has taken on for him. To use a term introduced in the discussion of the personal essay on page 26, the description is highly **subjective.**

(d) *What prompts the recollection that leads to thoughts of running off to sea? To put the question more generally, how has the author unified a long paragraph containing a description of the landscape and thoughts of going off to sea?*

yet craved, to the extent of public supplication, for the sympathetic cooperation of youths as apprentices. I did not rightly know what apprentices might be, nor whether I was yet big enough to be styled a youth; but one thing seemed clear, that, by some such means as this, whatever the intervening hardships, I could eventually visit all the circuses of the world— the circuses of merry France and gaudy Spain, of Holland and Bohemia, of China and Peru. Here was a plan worth thinking out in all its bearings; for something had presently to be done to end this intolerable state of things.

[10] Midday, and even feeding time, passed by gloomily enough, till a small disturbance occurred which had the effect of releasing some of the electricity with which the air was charged. Harold, it should be explained, was of a very different mental mold, and never brooded, moped, nor ate his heart out over any disappointment. One wild outburst—one dissolution of a minute into his original elements of air and water, of tears and outcry—so much insulted nature claimed. Then he would pull himself together, iron out his countenance with a smile, and adjust himself to the new condition of things.

[11] If the gods are ever grateful to man for anything, it is when he is so good as to display a short memory. The Olympians were never slow to recognize this quality of Harold's, in which, indeed, their salvation lay, and on this occasion their gratitude had taken the practical form of a fine fat orange, tough-rinded as oranges of those days were wont to be. This he had eviscerated in the good old-fashioned manner, by biting out a hole in the shoulder, inserting a lump of sugar therein, and then working it cannily till the whole soul and body of the orange passed glorified through the sugar

[10] The paragraph opens with a sentence that straightforwardly accounts for the passage of time and suggests the significance of an event that is to be told after we have been given further analysis of Harold's character. Thus the first sentence helps the pace of the narrative by keeping alive our interest in the progress of events.

[11] *How is the use of "Olympians" justified by the point of view of paragraphs 1, 2, and 6?*

into his being. Thereupon, filled full of orange juice and iniquity, he conceived a deadly snare. Having deftly patted and squeezed the orange skin till it resumed its original shape, he filled it up with water, inserted a fresh lump of sugar in the orifice, and, issuing forth, blandly proffered it to me as I sat moodily in the doorway dreaming of strange wild circuses under tropic skies.

12 Such a stale old dodge as this would hardly have taken me in at ordinary moments. But Harold had reckoned rightly upon the disturbing effect of ill-humor, and had guessed, perhaps, that I thirsted for comfort and consolation, and would not criticize too closely the source from which they came. Unthinkingly, I grasped the golden fraud, which collapsed at my touch, and squirted its contents into my eyes and over my collar, till the nethermost parts of me were damp with the water that had run down my neck. In an instant I had Harold down, and, with all the energy of which I was capable, devoted myself to grinding his head into the gravel; while, he, realizing that the closure was applied, and that the time for discussion or argument was past, sternly concentrated his powers on kicking me in the stomach.

12 Observe another instance of what should now be a familiar transitional device, here strengthened by the use of "such."

13 Some people can never allow events to work themselves out quietly. At this juncture one of Them swooped down on the scene, pouring shrill, misplaced abuse on both of us: on me for ill-treating my younger brother, whereas it was distinctly I who was the injured and the deceived; on him for the high offense of assault and battery on a clean collar—a collar which I had myself deflowered and defaced, shortly before, in sheer desperate ill-temper. Disgusted and defiant we fled in different directions, rejoining each other later in the kitchen garden; and as we strolled along together, our

13 *The capitalization of "Them" echoes what?*

This device may seem trivial, but any device that makes it possible for the writer to suggest his central theme repeatedly but unobrusively is a valuable means of achieving coherence and emphasis.

short feud forgotten, Harold observed, gloomily: "I should like to be a caveman, like Uncle George was tellin' us about: with a flint hatchet and no clothes, and live in a cave and not know anybody!"

14 "And if anyone came to see us we didn't like," I joined in, catching on to the points of the idea, "we'd hit him on the head with the hatchet till he dropped down dead."

14, 15 *How old do the boys seem to be?*

15 "And then," said Harold, warming up, "we'd drag him into the cave and *skin him!*"

16 For a space we gloated silently over the fair scene our imaginations had conjured up. It was *blood* we felt the need of just then. We wanted no luxuries, nothing dear-bought nor farfetched. Just plain blood, and nothing else, and plenty of it.

16, 17, 18 These paragraphs make a unit. Note that the references to "blood" tie paragraphs 17 and 18 together and the idea, though not the word, carries over into paragraph 19.

17 Blood, however, was not to be had. The time was out of joint, and we had been born too late. So we went off to the greenhouse, crawled into the heating arrangement underneath, and played at the dark and dirty and unrestricted life of cavemen till we were heartily sick of it. Then we emerged once more into historic times, and went off to the road to look for something living and sentient to throw stones at.

18 Nature, so often a cheerful ally, sometimes sulks and refuses to play. When in this mood she passes the word to her underlings, and all the little people of fur and feather take the hint and slip home quietly by back streets. In vain we scouted, lurked, crept, and ambuscaded. Everything that usually scurried, hopped, or fluttered—the small society of the undergrowth —seemed to have engagements elsewhere. The horrid thought that perhaps they had all gone off to the circus occurred to us simultaneously,

18 Note that the boys do not forget, and that the author does not permit the reader to forget, the disappointment over the circus.

and we humped ourselves up on the fence and felt bad. Even the sound of approaching wheels failed to stir any interest in us. When you are bent on throwing stones at something, humanity seems obtrusive and better away. Then suddenly we both jumped off the fence together, our faces clearing. For our educated ear had told us that the approaching rattle could only proceed from a dogcart, and we felt sure it must be the funny man.

[19] We called him the funny man because he was sad and serious, and said little, but gazed right into our souls, and made us tell him just what was on our minds at the time, and then came out with some magnificently luminous suggestion that cleared every cloud away. What was more, he would then go off with us at once and play the thing right out to its finish, earnestly and devotedly, putting all other things aside. So we called him the funny man, meaning only that he was different from those others who thought it incumbent on them to play the painful mummer. The ideal as opposed to the real man was what we meant, only we were not acquainted with the phrase. Those others, with their labored jests and clumsy contortions, doubtless flattered themselves that *they* were funny men; we, who had to sit through and applaud the painful performance, knew better.

[20] He pulled up to a walk as soon as he caught sight of us, and the dogcart crawled slowly along till it stopped just opposite. Then he leant his chin on his hand and regarded us long and soulfully, yet said he never a word; while we jigged up and down in the dust, grinning bashfully but with expectation. For you never knew exactly what this man might say or do.

[21] "You look bored," he remarked presently; "thoroughly bored. Or else—let me see; you're not married, are you?"

[19] This is a paragraph of **definition;** its purpose is to explain a term, in this case the childish use of a term that would be misunderstood if left undefined. The definition begins with a **paradox,** an apparently contradictory statement. As is usually true when paradoxes are deliberately employed, the contradiction is resolved, or disappears, once the terms of the statement are properly understood.

(a) *What method of development is used to explain what the narrator means by "funny man"?*
(b) *What quality has the "funny man" that makes him differ not only from the "painful mummer" but from the Olympians as well?*

COMPOSITION ASSIGNMENT

Write a paragraph of developed definition. Choose a term that is not commonly understood and for which dictionary definition is not adequate— a word or phrase used in a special sense by such a group as a family, a neighborhood gang, a particular profession, or persons associated in some other specialized activity. Develop the paragraph by giving an example or examples of the kind of person or thing to which the term applies. Remember the usefulness of comparison and contrast in suggesting the precise nature of the subject.

[20]–[27] These paragraphs show the important principle of offering specific

[22] He asked this in such sad earnestness that we hastened to assure him we were not married, though we felt he ought to have known that much; we had been intimate for some time.

[23] "Then it's only boredom," he said. "Just satiety and world-weariness. Well, if you assure me you aren't married you can climb into this cart and I'll take you for a drive. I'm bored, too. I want to do something dark and dreadful and exciting."

[24] We clambered in, of course, yapping with delight and treading all over his toes; and as we set off, Harold demanded of him imperiously whither he was going.

[25] "My wife," he replied, "has ordered me to go and look up the curate and bring him home to tea. Does that sound sufficiently exciting for you?"

[26] Our faces fell. The curate of the hour was not a success, from our point of view. He was not a funny man, in any sense of the word.

[27] "—But I'm not going to," he added, cheerfully. "Then I was to stop at some cottage and ask—what was it? There was *nettle rash* mixed up in it, I'm sure. But never mind, I've forgotten, and it doesn't matter. Look here, we're three desperate young fellows who stick at nothing. Suppose we go off to the circus?"

[28] Of certain supreme moments it is not easy to write. The varying shades and currents of emotion may indeed be put into words by those specially skilled that way; they often are, at considerable length. But the sheer, crude article itself—the strong, live thing that leaps up inside you and swells and strangles you, the dizziness of revulsion that takes the breath like cold

details in **illustration** of what has been asserted, or said to be true. They clarify and support the preceding characterization of the funny man. We observe him and hear him instead of merely being told about him.

How do these paragraphs help us to understand the paradox of paragraph 19?

[28]–[36] This sequence of paragraphs presents the climactic **episode** of the narrative.

First read through the entire sequence and then make a paragraph by paragraph analysis. Determine the topic idea of each paragraph and make any observations that you can on the means used to develop it. Try to make a definite statement about the part played by each paragraph in the development of the whole. Point out transitions between and within paragraphs.

water—who shall depict this and live? All I knew was that I would have died then and there, cheerfully, for the funny man; that I longed for red Indians to spring out from the hedge on the dogcart, just to show what I would do; and that, with all this, I could not find the least little word to say to him.

[29] Harold was less taciturn. With shrill voice, uplifted in solemn chant, he sang the great spheral circus-song, and the undying glory of the Ring. Of its timeless beginning he sang, of its fashioning by cosmic forces, and of its harmony with the stellar plan. Of horses he sang, of their strength, their swiftness, and their docility as to tricks. Of clowns again, of the glory of knavery, and of the eternal type that shall endure. Lastly he sang of Her—the Woman of the Ring—flawless, complete, untrammeled in each subtly curving limb; earth's highest output, time's noblest expression. At least, he doubtless sang all these things and more—he certainly seemed to; though all that was distinguishable was, "We're-goin'-to-the-circus!" and then, once more, "We're-goin'-to-the-circus!"—the sweet rhythmic phrase repeated again and again. But indeed I cannot be quite sure, for I heard confusedly, as in a dream. Wings of fire sprang from the old mare's shoulders. We whirled on our way through purple clouds, and earth and the rattle of wheels were far away below.

[30] The dream and the dizziness were still in my head when I found myself, scarce conscious of intermediate steps, seated actually in the circus at last, and took in the first sniff of that intoxicating circus smell that will stay by me while this clay endures. The place was beset by a hum and a glitter and a mist; suspense brooded large o'er the blank, mysterious arena.

Strung up to the highest pitch of expectation, we knew not from what quarter, in what divine shape, the first surprise would come.

31 A thud of unseen hoofs first set us a-quiver; then a crash of cymbals, a jangle of bells, a hoarse applauding roar, and Coralie was in the midst of us, whirling past 'twixt earth and sky, now erect, flushed, radiant, now crouched to the flowing mane; swung and tossed and molded by the maddening dance music of the band. The mighty whip of the count in the frock coat marked time with pistol shots; his war cry, whooping clear above the music, fired the blood with a passion for splendid deeds, as Coralie, laughing, exultant, crashed through the paper hoops. We gripped the red cloth in front of us, and our souls sped round and round with Coralie, leaping with her, prone with her, swung by mane or tail with her. It was not only the ravishment of her delirious feats, nor her cream-colored horse of fairy breed, long-tailed, roe-footed, an enchanted prince surely, if ever there was one! It was her more than mortal beauty—displayed, too, under conditions never vouchsafed to us before—that held us spellbound. What princess had arms so dazzlingly white, or went delicately clothed in such pink and spangles? Hitherto we had known the outward woman as but a drab thing, hour-glass shaped, nearly legless, bunched here, constricted there; slow of movement, and given to deprecating lusty action of limb. Here was a revelation! From henceforth our imaginations would have to be revised and corrected up to date. In one of those swift rushes the mind makes in high-strung moments, I saw myself and Coralie, close enfolded, pacing the world together, o'er hill and plain, through storied cities, past rows of applauding relations—I in my Sunday knickerbockers, she in her pink and spangles.

[32]   Summers sicken, flowers fail and die, all beauty but rides round the ring and out at the portal; even so Coralie passed in her turn, poised sideways, panting, on her steed; lightly swayed as a tulip bloom, bowing on this side and on that as she disappeared; and with her went my heart and my soul, and all the light and the glory and the entrancement of the scene.

[33]   Harold woke up with a gasp. "Wasn't she beautiful?" he said, in quite a subdued way for him. I felt a momentary pang. We had been friendly rivals before, in many an exploit; but here was altogether a more serious affair. Was this, then, to be the beginning of strife and coldness, of civil war on the hearthstone and the sundering of old ties? Then I recollected the true position of things, and felt very sorry for Harold; for it was inexorably written that he would have to give way to me, since I was the elder. Rules were not made for nothing, in a sensibly constructed universe.

[34]   There was little more to wait for, now Coralie had gone; yet I lingered still, on the chance of her appearing again. Next moment the clown tripped up and fell flat, with magnificent artifice, and at once fresh emotions began to stir. Love had endured its little hour, and stern ambition now asserted itself. Oh, to be a splendid fellow like this, self-contained, ready of speech, agile beyond conception, braving the forces of society, his hand against everyone, yet always getting the best of it! What freshness of humor, what courtesy to dames, what triumphant ability to discomfit rivals, frock-coated and mustached though they might be! And what a grand, self-confident straddle of the legs! Who could desire a finer career than to go through life thus gorgeously equipped! Success was his keynote, adroitness his panoply, and the

mellow music of laughter his instant reward. Even Coralie's image wavered and receded. I would come back to her in the evening, of course; but I would be a clown all the working hours of the day.

35 The short interval was ended: the band, with long-drawn chords, sounded a prelude touched with significance; and the program, in letters overtopping their fellows, proclaimed Zephyrine, the Bride of the Desert, in her unequaled bareback equestrian interlude. So sated was I already with beauty and with wit, that I hardly dared hope for a fresh emotion. Yet her title was tinged with romance, and Coralie's display had aroused in me an interest in her sex which even herself had failed to satisfy entirely.

36 Brayed in by trumpets, Zephyrine swung passionately into the arena. With a bound she stood erect, one foot upon each of her supple, plunging Arabs; and at once I knew that my fate was sealed, my chapter closed, and the Bride of the Desert was the one bride for me. Black was her raiment, great silver stars shone through it, caught in the dusky twilight of her gauze; black as her own hair were the two mighty steeds she bestrode. In a tempest they thundered by, in a whirlwind, a *sirocco* of tan; her cheeks bore the kiss of an Eastern sun, and the sandstorms of her native desert were her satellites. What was Coralie, with her pink silk, her golden hair and slender limbs, beside this magnificent, full-figured Cleopatra? In a twinkling we were scouring the desert—she and I and two coal-black horses. Side by side, keeping pace in our swinging gallop, we distanced the ostrich, we outstrode the zebra; and, as we went, it seemed the wilderness blossomed like the rose.

[37] I know not rightly how we got home that evening. On the road there were everywhere strange presences, and the thud of phantom hoofs encircled us. In my nose was the pungent circus smell; the crack of the whip and the frank laugh of the clown were in my ears. The funny man thoughtfully abstained from conversation, and left our illusion quite alone, sparing us all jarring criticism and analysis; and he gave me no chance, when he deposited us at our gate, to get rid of the clumsy expressions of gratitude I had been laboriously framing. For the rest of the evening, distraught and silent, I only heard the march music of the band, playing on in some corner of my brain. When at last my head touched the pillow, in a trice I was with Zephyrine, riding the boundless Sahara, cheek to cheek, the world well lost; while at times, through the sandclouds that encircled us, glimmered the eyes of Coralie, touched, one fancied, with something of a tender reproach.

[37] This paragraph serves as a natural conclusion of the essay, for most readers can recall what it is like for a child to come home at night full of recollections of a special outing.

Are all the details of this paragraph in keeping with your own recollections of similar situations, or are there some that do not ring true?

SUMMARY

Consider the effectiveness of the essay as a whole. Is the major theme of the essay the carelessness of parents or the magic of the circus? Which of these themes is developed in a more imaginative manner? Is the essay effectively unified?

The concluding section of "The Magic Ring," paragraphs 29–36, may raise questions of appropriateness of language. Throughout the essay, Kenneth Grahame has presented his recollections of childhood from the point of view of a child, but we can see that he has not limited himself to the language of a child. Some may feel that the descriptions of the child's recollections of the circus are excessively lavish, elaborately fanciful and romantic, even flowery or highflown. Furthermore, regardless of the language in which they are expressed, some of the observations and concerns may not seem characteristic of a boy of the narrator's apparent age (see page 33, paragraphs 14 and 15). The question is whether the choice of language is justified by a persuasive interpretation of the attitudes of the boy.

Compare the language of the concluding section with that of the excerpt from Mark Twain's *Huckleberry Finn* printed below. What differences do you observe?

It was a real bully circus. It was the splendidest sight that ever was when they all come riding in, two and two, and gentleman and lady, side by side, the men just in their drawers and undershirts, and no shoes nor stirrups, and resting their hands on their thighs easy and comfortable—there must a been twenty of them—and every lady with a lovely complexion, and perfectly beautiful, and looking just like a gang of real sure-enough queens, and dressed in clothes that cost millions of dollars, and just littered with diamonds. It was a powerful fine sight; I never see anything so lovely. And then one by one they got up and stood, and went a-weaving around the ring so gentle and wavy and graceful, the men looking ever so tall and airy and straight, with their heads bobbing and skimming along, away up there under the tent roof, and every lady's rose-leafy dress flapping soft and silky around her hips, and she looking like the most loveliest parasol.

And then faster and faster they went, all of them dancing, first one foot out in the air and then the other, the horses leaning more and more, and the ringmaster going round and round the center pole, cracking his whip and shouting "Hi!—hi!" and the clown cracking jokes behind him; and by and by all hands dropped the reins, and every lady put her knuckles on her hips and every gentleman folded his arms, and then how the horses did lean over and hump themselves. And so one after the other they all skipped off into the ring, and made the sweetest bow I ever see, and then scampered out, and everybody clapped their hands and went just about wild.

COMPOSITION ASSIGNMENT

Recall an experience you had some years ago in which a longing or desire you had was fulfilled or frustrated. Then write a narrative essay in which you reveal the feelings that the experience aroused in you. Take special care with the transitions.

NARRATIVE-DESCRIPTIVE WRITING

3 | *Narrative-Descriptive Writing*

To maintain too rigidly the distinction between the different types of the essay is artificial because they seldom, if ever, exist as pure forms. As noted in Section 2, description plays an important part in essays classified as basically narrative. The essays of Section 3 use a chronology of events as the basis for presenting descriptive detail. The difference is one of purpose: whereas in Section 2 the narrative interest predominates, in the essays of Section 3 the author's chief intention is to give us his impression of a setting and of the events which he observes.

A NIGHT AMONG THE PINES

Robert Louis Stevenson

This essay, from *Travels with a Donkey*, is a well-known narrative-descriptive work in which Stevenson gives an account of a night he spent camping in the woods during a trip he made in the south of France. The essay moves in time and various things happen; thus it is narrative in structure. However, the main interest in the essay is the series of impressions which Stevenson records; thus it is basically descriptive.

[1] From Bleymard after dinner, although it was already late, I set out to scale a portion of the Lozere. An ill-marked stony drove-road guided me forward, and I met nearly half a dozen bullock carts descending from the woods, each laden with a whole pine tree for the winter's firing. At the top of the woods, which do not climb very high upon this cold ridge, I struck leftward by a path among the pines, until I hit on a dell of green turf, where a streamlet made a little spout over some stones to serve for a water tap. "In a more sacred or sequestered bower . . . nor nymph, nor faunus, haunted." The trees were not old, but they grew thickly round the glade: there was no outlook, except northeastward upon distant hilltops, or straight upward to the sky; and the encampment felt secure and private like a room. By the time I had made my arrangements and fed Modestine, the day was already beginning to decline. I buckled myself to the knees into my sack and made a hearty meal; and as soon as the sun went down, I pulled my cap over my eyes and fell asleep.

[1] This paragraph is narrative introduction. It tells of the author's trip up the mountain, his discovery of a suitable spot to spend the night, and his making camp.

2 Night is a dead monotonous period under a roof; but in the open world it passes lightly, with its stars and dews and perfumes, and the hours are marked by changes in the face of Nature. What seems a kind of temporal death to people choked between walls and curtains, is only a light and living slumber to the man who sleeps afield. All night long he can hear Nature breathing deeply and freely; even as she takes her rest, she turns and smiles; and there is one stirring hour unknown to those who dwell in houses, when a wakeful influence goes abroad over the sleeping hemisphere, and all the outdoor world are on their feet. It is then that the cock first crows, not this time to announce the dawn, but like a cheerful watchman speeding the course of night. Cattle awake on the meadows; sheep break their fast on dewy hillsides, and change to a new lair among the ferns; and houseless men, who have lain down with the fowls, open their dim eyes and behold the beauty of the night.

3 At what inaudible summons, at what gentle touch of Nature, are all these sleepers thus recalled in the same hour to life? Do the stars rain down an influence, or do we share some thrill of mother earth below our resting bodies? Even shepherds and old countryfolk, who are the deepest read in these arcana, have not a guess as to the means or purpose of this nightly resurrection. Towards two in the morning they declare the thing takes place; and neither know nor inquire further. And at least it is a pleasant incident. We are disturbed in our slumber only, like the luxurious Montaigne,* "that we

2 This paragraph begins with a personal observation: night under a roof is dead and monotonous; in the open, it is alive.

(a) *How is the idea developed?*
(b) *What is the function of the series of main clauses composing the last sentence? In other words, what is the function of the* **structure** *of the sentence?*

3 (a) *What do the questions which introduce the paragraph add to what has already been said?*
(b) *What is the allusion in the first part of the paragraph?*

---

* *Montaigne:* Michel Eyquem de Montaigne (1533–1592). A French nobleman who first used the word *essai* (from the French verb *essayer*, meaning "to try") to designate a form of writing in which an idea or experience is discussed in a personal style. In one such *essai*, he describes the pleasure he gains from having a servant wake him in the middle of the night to tell him that he has hours more to sleep.

may the better and more sensibly relish it." We have a moment to look upon the stars, and there is a special pleasure for some minds in the reflection that we share the impulse with all outdoor creatures in our neighborhood, that we have escaped out of the bastille of civilization, and are become, for the time being, a mere kindly animal and a sheep of Nature's flock.

(c) *"Bastille" introduces a metaphor as well as an allusion. What is implied by the metaphor?*

4 When that hour came to me among the pines, I wakened thirsty. My tin was standing by me half full of water. I emptied it at a draft; and feeling broad awake after this internal cold aspersion, sat upright to make a cigarette. The stars were clear, colored, and jewel-like, but not frosty. A faint silvery vapor stood for the Milky Way. All around me the black fir points stood upright and stock-still. By the whiteness of the packsaddle, I could see Modestine walking round and round at the length of her tether; I could hear her steadily munching at the sward; but there was not another sound, save the indescribably quiet talk of the runnel over the stones. I lay lazily smoking and studying the color of the sky, as we call the void of space, from where it showed a reddish gray behind the pines to where it showed a glossy blue-black between the stars. As if to be more like a pedlar, I wear a silver ring. This I could see faintly shining as I raised or lowered the cigarette, and at each whiff the inside of my hand was illuminated, and became for a second the highest light in the landscape.

4 This paragraph begins with a transitional sentence and after some narrative continues as a descriptive paragraph.

(a) *What impression is created?*
(b) *List the details which give this impression.*
(c) *What determines the order or sequence of the details?*

5 A faint wind, more like a moving coolness than a stream of air, passed down the glade from time to time; so that even in my great chamber the air was being renewed all night long. I thought with horror of the inn at Chasseradès and the congregated nightcaps; with horror of the nocturnal prowesses of clerks and students, of hot theaters and passkeys and close

5 After a descriptive transition, the paragraph develops an impression by contrast.

(a) *What is the impression?*
(b) *What exactly is contrasted with what?*
(c) *The paragraph ends with a qualifying thought. What is it?*

rooms. I have not often enjoyed a more serene possession of myself, nor felt more independent of material aids. The outer world, from which we cower into our houses, seemed after all a gentle habitable place; and night after night a man's bed, it seemed, was laid and waiting for him in the fields, where God keeps an open house. I thought I had rediscovered one of those truths which are revealed to savages and hid from political economists: at the least, I had discovered a new pleasure for myself. And yet even while I was exulting in my solitude I became aware of a strange lack. I wished a companion to lie near me in the starlight, silent and not moving, but ever within touch. For there is a fellowship more quiet even than solitude, and which, rightly understood, is solitude made perfect. And to live out of doors with the woman a man loves is of all lives the most complete and free.

6   As I thus lay, between content and longing, a faint noise stole towards me through the pines. I thought, at first, it was the crowing of cocks or the barking of dogs at some very distant farm; but steadily and gradually it took articulate shape in my ears, until I became aware that a passenger was going by upon the highroad in the valley, and singing loudly as he went. There was more of good will than grace in his performance; but he trolled with ample lungs; and the sound of his voice took hold upon the hillside and set the air shaking in the leafy glens. I have heard people passing by night in sleeping cities; some of them sang; one, I remember, played loudly on the bagpipes. I have heard the rattle of a cart or carriage spring up suddenly after hours of stillness, and pass, for some minutes, within the range of my hearing as I lay abed. There is a romance about all who are abroad in the black hours, and with something

6 **(a)** *How does Stevenson achieve the transition from paragraph 5?*
(b) *What is the topic sentence?*
(c) *Why is it placed where it is?*

of a thrill we try to guess their business. But here the romance was double: first, this glad passenger lit internally with wine, who sent up his voice in music through the night; and then I, on the other hand, buckled into my sack, and smoking alone in the pine woods between four and five thousand feet towards the stars.

[7]   When I awoke again (Sunday, 29th September), many of the stars had disappeared; only the stronger companions of the night still burned visibly overhead; and away towards the east I saw a faint haze of light upon the horizon, such as had been the Milky Way when I was last awake. Day was at hand. I lit my lantern, and by its glowworm light put on my boots and gaiters; then I broke up some bread for Modestine, filled my can at the water tap, and lit my spirit lamp to boil myself some chocolate. The blue darkness lay long in the glade where I had so sweetly slumbered; but soon there was a broad streak of orange melting into gold along the mountain tops of Vivarais. A solemn glee possessed my mind at this gradual and lovely coming in of day. I heard the runnel with delight; I looked round me for something beautiful and unexpected; but the still, black pine trees, the hollow glade, the munching ass, remained unchanged in figure. Nothing had altered but the light, and that, indeed, shed over all a spirit of life and of breathing peace, and moved me to a strange exhilaration.

[8]   I drank my water chocolate, which was hot if it was not rich, and strolled here and there, and up and down about the glade. While I was thus delaying, a gush of steady wind, as long as a heavy sigh, poured direct out of the quarter of the morning. It was cold, and set me sneezing. The trees near at hand tossed their black plumes in its passage; and I could see the

[7], [8]   Both paragraphs deal with the gradual coming of day.

(a) *What is the transition between paragraphs 6 and 7?*
(b) *Why are there two separate paragraphs instead of one?*
(c) *Explain the paradox of "solemn glee."*
(d) *What method of development is used in both paragraphs?*

thin, distant spires of pine along the edge of the hill rock slightly to and fro against the golden east. Ten minutes after, the sunlight spread at a gallop along the hillsides, scattering shadows and sparkles, and then day had come completely.

9   I hastened to prepare my pack, and tackle the steep ascent that lay before me; but I had something on my mind. It was only a fancy; yet a fancy will sometimes be importunate. I had been most hospitably received and punctually served in my green caravanserai. The room was airy, the water excellent, and the dawn had called me to a moment. I say nothing of the tapestries or the inimitable ceiling, nor yet of the view which I commanded from the windows; but I felt I was in someone's debt for all this liberal entertainment. And so it pleased me, in a half-laughing way, to leave pieces of money on the turf as I went along, until I had left enough for my night's lodging. I trust they did not fall to some rich and churlish drover.

9   The essay ends with a fanciful comparison.

(a) *What is being compared and why?*
(b) *How does this comparison differ from a metaphor?*

COMPOSITION ASSIGNMENT

Write a narrative-descriptive essay based on your own experience. You may describe some hiking, camping, or sailing trip. If you have had no such experience, you might describe a visit to the city or other place of interest. Your composition should be a personal essay, not a report. In other words, you should avoid a detailed account of what happened and use the narrative as a framework for your main concern—the impression made upon you by the experience.

THE MOWING OF A FIELD

Hilaire Belloc

This essay is a rather complex combination of exposition, narration, and description. It opens with a description of a valley in South England. To this valley the narrator returns after a long absence. The main part of the essay is devoted to the day spent by the narrator mowing his field in the valley. As he deals with the mowing, Belloc introduces a number of thoughts which are suggested by the mowing but which are not an integral part of it. In these seeming digressions lies a large part of the appeal of the essay; they make it a personal essay rather than a report.

1 There is a valley in South England remote from ambition and from fear, where the passage of strangers is rare and unperceived, and where the scent of the grass in summer is breathed only by those who are native to that unvisited land. The roads to the Channel do not traverse it; they choose upon either side easier passes over the range. One track alone leads up through it to the hills, and this is changeable: now green where men have little occasion to go, now a good road where it nears the homesteads and the barns. The woods grow steep above the slopes; they reach sometimes the very summit of the heights, or, when they cannot attain them, fill in and clothe the coombes. And, in between, along the floor of the valley, deep pastures and their silence are bordered by lawns of chalky grass and the small yew trees of the downs.

1 (a) *What is the topic idea of the paragraph?*
(b) *How are details used to develop the idea?*

[2] The clouds that visit its sky reveal themselves beyond the one great rise, and sail, white and enormous, to the other, and sink beyond that other. But the plains above which they have traveled and the weald to which they go, the people of the valley cannot see and hardly recall. The wind, when it reaches such fields, is no longer a gale from the salt, but fruitful and soft, an inland breeze; and those whose blood was nourished here feel in that wind the fruitfulness of our orchards and all the life that all things draw from the air.

[2] (a) *How does the topic idea of this paragraph differ from that of paragraph 1?*
(b) *How is the transition achieved?*

[3] In this place, when I was a boy, I pushed through a fringe of beeches that made a complete screen between me and the world, and I came to a glade called No Man's Land. I climbed beyond it, and I was surprised and glad, because from the ridge of that glade, I saw the sea. To this place very lately I returned.

[3] This is a transitional paragraph.

(a) *It accomplishes a transition from what to what?*
(b) *Which sentence is most important in the transition? Why?*

[4] The many things that I recovered as I came up the countryside were not less charming than when a distant memory had enshrined them, but much more. Whatever veil is thrown by a longing recollection had not intensified nor even made more mysterious the beauty of that happy ground; not in my very dreams of morning had I, in exile, seen it more beloved or more rare. Much also that I had forgotten now returned to me as I approached—a group of elms, a little turn of the parson's wall, a small paddock beyond the graveyard close, cherished by one man, with a low wall of very old stone guarding it all round. And all these things fulfilled and amplified my delight, till even the good vision of the place, which I had kept so many years, left me and was replaced by its better reality. "Here," I said to myself, "is a symbol of what some say is reserved for the soul: pleasure of a kind which cannot be imagined save in a moment when at last it is attained."

[4] This is basically a paragraph of comparison.

(a) *What two things are compared?*
(b) *What is the conclusion of the comparison?*

The words "enshrined," "veil," and "exile" are metaphoric in this context. Here "enshrined" implies the comparison of the countryside to a shrine. "Shrine" suggests holiness and worship. Belloc implies that through his memory he has worshipped the various objects in the countryside.

(c) *What do "veil" and "exile" add by way of suggestion to the statement of fact?*

⑤ When I came to my own gate and my own field, and had before me the house I knew, I looked around a little (though it was already evening), and I saw that the grass was standing as it should stand when it is ready for the scythe. For in this, as in everything that a man can do— of those things at least which are very old— there is an exact moment when they are done best. And it has been remarked of whatever rules us that it works blunderingly, seeing that the good things given to a man are not given at the precise moment when they would have filled him with delight. But, whether this be true or false, we can choose the just turn of the seasons in everything we do of our own will, and especially in the making of hay. Many think that hay is best made when the grass is thickest; and so they delay until it is rank and in flower, and has already heavily pulled the ground. And there is another false reason for delay, which is wet weather. For very few will understand (though it comes year after year) that we have rain always in South England between the sickle and the scythe, or say just after the weeks of east wind are over. First we have a week of sudden warmth, as though the South had come to see us all; then we have the weeks of east and southeast wind; and then we have more or less of that rain of which I spoke, and which always astonishes the world. Now it is just before, or during, or at the very end of that rain—but not later—that grass should be cut for hay. True, upland grass, which is always thin, should be cut earlier than the grass in the bottoms and along the water meadows; but not even the latest, even in the wettest seasons, should be left (as it is) to flower and even to seed. For what we get when we store our grass is not a harvest of something ripe, but a thing just caught in its prime before maturity: as witness that our corn and straw are best yellow, but our hay is best green. So also Death

⑤ This paragraph contains the first of many digressions. It is an interesting combination of abstract statements about life and concrete details about the proper time for haying.

(a) *What sentences present the abstract ideas?*
(b) *Why should "Death be represented with a scythe and Time with a sickle"?*

should be represented with a scythe and Time with a sickle; for Time can take only what is ripe, but Death comes always too soon. In a word, then, it is always much easier to cut grass too late than too early; and I, under that evening and come back to these pleasant fields, looked at the grass and knew that it was time. June was in full advance: it was the beginning of that season when the night has already lost her foothold of the earth and hovers over it, never quite descending, but mixing sunset with the dawn.

6 Next morning, before it was yet broad day, I awoke, and thought of the mowing. The birds were already chattering in the trees beside my window, all except the nightingale, which had left and flown away to the weald, where he sings all summer by day as well as by night in the oaks and the hazel spinneys, and especially along the little river Adur, one of the rivers of the weald. The birds and the thought of the mowing had awakened me, and I went down the stairs and along the stone floors to where I could find a scythe; and when I took it from its nail, I remembered how, fourteen years ago, I had last gone out with my scythe, just so, into the fields at morning. In between that day and this were many things, cities and armies, and a confusion of books, mountains and the desert, and horrible great breadths of sea.

6 The first sentence is a narrative transition involving time sequence. The last sentence returns to the comparison of past and present. The series with which the sentence ends is not a simple listing of separate items.

Can you see why Belloc has grouped the items of the series as he has?

7 When I got out into the long grass the sun was not yet risen, but there were already many colors in the eastern sky, and I made haste to sharpen my scythe, so that I might get to the cutting before the dew should dry. Some say that it is best to wait till all the dew has risen, so as to get the grass quite dry from the very first. But, though it is an advantage to get the

7 (a) *What is the topic of the paragraph?*
(b) *What is the basic method of development?*
(c) *What is the function of the last sentence?*

55

grass quite dry, yet it is not worth while to wait till the dew has risen. For, in the first place, you lose many hours of work (and those the coolest), and next—which is more important— you lose that great ease and thickness in cutting which comes of the dew. So I at once began to sharpen my scythe.

[8] There is an art also in the sharpening of the scythe, and it is worth describing carefully. Your blade must be dry, and that is why you will see men rubbing the scythe blade with grass before they whet it. Then also your rubber must be quite dry, and on this account it is a good thing to lay it on your coat and keep it there during all your day's mowing. The scythe you stand upright, with the blade pointing away from you, and put your left hand firmly on the back of the blade, grasping it; then you pass the rubber first down one side of the blade edge and then down the other, beginning near the handle and going on to the point and work- ing quickly and hard. When you first do this you will, perhaps, cut your hand; but it is only at first that such an accident will happen to you.

[9] To tell when the scythe is sharp enough this is the rule. First the stone clangs and grinds against the iron harshly; then it rings musically to one note; then, at last, it purrs as though the iron and stone were exactly suited. When you hear this, your scythe is sharp enough; and I, when I heard it that June dawn, with every- thing quite silent except the birds, let down the scythe and bent myself to mow.

[10] When one does anything anew, after so many years, one fears very much for one's trick or habit. But all things once learnt are easily recoverable, and I very soon recovered the swing and power of the mower. Mowing

[8], [9]   Taken by themselves these paragraphs are exposition of the most practical kind: the clear statement of a process, in this case the sharpening of a scythe. A process has a beginning, a middle, and an end and is generally—as in this instance— presented chronologically.

(a) *Mark off the stages of the process.*
(b) *Pick out the transitional words.*
(c) *How are these words related to the method of paragraph development?*
(d) *What does the inclusion of this practical information contribute to the theme of the essay as a whole?*
(e) *Again, what is the function of the last sentence in paragraph 9?*

[10]   This is also an expository paragraph; it is devoted to the proper method of mowing.

(a) *How is the paragraph developed?*
(b) *How does the sentence structure of the section which deals with the actions of the unskilled mower differ from that of the section which describes the actions of the "good mower"?*

well and mowing badly—or rather not mowing at all—are separated by very little; as is also true of writing verse, or playing the fiddle, and of dozens of other things, but of nothing more than of believing. For the bad or young or untaught mower without tradition, the mower Promethean, the mower original and contemptuous of the past, does all these things: he leaves great crescents of grass uncut. He digs the point of the scythe hard into the ground with a jerk. He loosens the handles and even the fastening of the blade. He twists the blade with his blunders, he blunts the blade, he chips it, dulls it, or breaks it clean off at the tip. If anyone is standing by he cuts him in the ankle. He sweeps up into the air wildly, with nothing to resist his stroke. He drags up earth with the grass, which is like making the meadow bleed. But the good mower who does things just as they should be done and have been for a hundred thousand years, falls into none of these fooleries. He goes foward very steadily, his scythe blade just barely missing the ground, every grass falling; the swish and rhythm of his mowing are always the same.

[11] So great an art can only be learnt by continual practice; but this much is worth writing down, that, as in all good work, to know the thing with which you work is the core of the affair. Good verse is best written on good paper with an easy pen, not with a lump of coal on a whitewashed wall. The pen thinks for you; and so does the scythe mow for you if you treat it honorably and in a manner that makes it recognize its service. The manner is this. You must regard the scythe as a pendulum that swings, not as a knife that cuts. A good mower puts no more strength into his stroke than into his lifting. Again, stand up to your work. The

[11] This paragraph continues the exposition of the art of mowing. In the process Belloc extends the principles of good mowing to other activities.

What are these activities, and what is the basis of the comparison?

bad mower, eager and full of pain, leans forward and tries to force the scythe through the grass. The good mower, serene and able, stands as nearly straight as the shape of the scythe will let him, and follows up every stroke closely, moving his left foot forward. Then also let every stroke get well away. Mowing is a thing of ample gestures, like drawing a cartoon. Then, again, get yourself into a mechanical and repetitive mood: be thinking of anything at all but your mowing, and be anxious only when there seems some interruption to the monotony of the sound. In this mowing should be like one's prayers—all of a sort and always the same, and so made that you can establish a monotony and work then, as it were, with half your mind: that happier half, the half that does not bother.

[12] In this way, when I had recovered the art after so many years, I went forward over the field, cutting lane after lane through the grass, and bringing out its most secret essences with the sweep of the scythe until the air was full of odors. At the end of every lane I sharpened my scythe and looked back at the work done, and then carried my scythe down again upon my shoulder to begin another. So, long before the bell rang in the chapel above me—that is, long before six o'clock, which is the time for the *Angelus*—I had many swathes already lying in order parallel like soldiery; and the high grass yet standing, making a great contrast with the shaven part, looked dense and high. As it says in the *Ballad of Val-es-Dunes*, where

> The tall son of the Seven Winds
> Came riding out of Hither-hythe,

and his horse-hoofs (you will remember) trampled into the press and made a gap in it,

[12] Here Belloc resumes the narrative. The paragraph also contains an appropriate quotation, a common device of the personal essay.

and his sword (as you know)

> was like a scythe
> In Arcus when the grass is high
> And all the swathes in order lie,
> And there's the bailiff standing by
> A-gathering of the tithe.

[13] So I mowed all that morning, till the houses awoke in the valley, and from some of them rose a little fragrant smoke, and men began to be seen.

[13], [14] These are short transitional paragraphs introducing the character of the English countryman.

[14] I stood still and rested on my scythe to watch the awakening of the village, when I saw coming up to my field a man whom I had known in older times, before I had left the Valley.

[14] *Why is paragraph 14 separate from paragraph 16?*

[15] He was of that dark silent race upon which all the learned quarrel, but which, by whatever meaningless name it may be called— Iberian, or Celtic, or what you will—is the permanent root of all England, and makes England wealthy and preserves it everywhere, except perhaps in the Fens and in a part of Yorkshire. Everywhere else you will find it active and strong. These people are intensive; their thoughts and their labors turn inward. It is on account of their presence in these islands that our gardens are the richest in the world. They also love low rooms and ample fires and great warm slopes of thatch. They have, as I believe, an older acquaintance with the English air than any other of all the strains that make up England. They hunted in the weald with stones, and camped in the pines of the greensand. They lurked under the oaks of the upper rivers, and saw the legionaries go up, up the straight paved road from the sea. They helped the few pirates to destroy the towns, and mixed

[15] This paragraph describes the English countryman.

(a) *Does it have a topic idea? If so, what?*
(b) *Does it have a topic sentence? If so, which?*
(c) *What method of development is used in the last half of the paragraph?*

with those pirates and shared the spoils of the Roman villas, and were glad to see the captains and the priests destroyed. They remain; and no admixture of the Frisian pirates, or the Breton, or the Angevin and Norman conquerors, has very much affected their cunning eyes.

[16] To this race, I say, belonged the man who now approached me. And he said to me, "Mowing?" And I answered, "Ar." Then he also said "Ar," as in duty bound; for so we speak to each other in the Stenes of the Downs.

[17] Next he told me that, as he had nothing to do, he would lend me a hand; and I thanked him warmly, or, as we say, "kindly." For it is a good custom of ours always to treat bargaining as though it were a courteous pastime; and though what he was after was money, and what I wanted was his labor at the least pay, yet we both played the comedy that we were free men, the one granting a grace and the other accepting it. For the dry bones of commerce, avarice and method and need, are odious to the Valley; and we cover them up with a pretty body of fiction and observances. Thus, when it comes to buying pigs, the buyer does not begin to decry the pig and the vendor to praise it, as is the custom with lesser men; but tradition makes them do business in this fashion:

[18] First the buyer will go up to the seller when he sees him in his own steading, and, looking at the pig with admiration, the buyer will say the rain may or may not fall, or that we shall have snow or thunder, according to the time of the year. Then the seller, looking critically at the pig, will agree that the weather is as his friend maintains. There is no haste at all; great leisure marks the dignity of their ex-

[17], [18] These two paragraphs consist of a stated idea illustrated by an **anecdote**—a short narrative used to clarify a general or abstract idea.

(a) *In these paragraphs, what is the main idea presented?*
(b) *How does the narrative support the idea?*

change. And the next step is, that the buyer says: "That's a fine pig you have there, Mr. ——" (giving the seller's name). "Ar, powerful fine pig." Then the seller, saying also "Mr." (for twin brothers rocked in one cradle give each other ceremonious observance here), the seller, I say, admits, as though with reluctance, the strength and beauty of the pig, and falls into deep thought. Then the buyer says, as though moved by a great desire, that he is ready to give so much for the pig, naming half the proper price, or a little less. Then the seller remains in silence for some moments; and at last begins to shake his head slowly, till he says: "I don't be thinking of selling the pig, anyways." He will also add that a party only Wednesday offered him so much for the pig—and he names about double the proper price. Thus all ritual is duly accomplished; and the solemn act is entered upon with reverence and in a spirit of truth. For when the buyer uses this phrase: "I'll tell you what I *will* do," and offers within half a crown of the pig's value; the difference is split, the pig is sold, and in the quiet soul of each runs the peace of something accomplished.

[19] Thus do we buy a pig or land or labor or malt or lime, always with elaboration and set forms; and many a London man has paid double and more for his violence and his greedy haste and very unchivalrous higgling. As happened with the land at Underwaltham, which the mortgagees had begged and implored the estate to take at twelve hundred, and had privately offered to all the world at a thousand, but which a sharp direct man, of the kind that makes great fortunes, a man in a motor-car, a man in a fur coat, a man of few words, bought for two thousand three hundred before my very eyes, protesting that they might take his offer or leave it; and all because he did not begin by praising the land.

[19] This paragraph consists of idea developed by anecdote on a smaller scale.

Again, what is the idea and how does the anecdote support it?

[20] Well then, this man I spoke of offered to help me, and he went to get his scythe. But I went into the house and brought out a gallon jar of small ale for him and for me; for the sun was now very warm, and small ale goes well with mowing. When we had drunk some of this ale in mugs called "I see you," we took each a swathe, he a little behind me because he was the better mower; and so for many hours we swung, one before the other, mowing and mowing at the tall grass of the field. And the sun rose to noon and we were still at our mowing; and we ate food, but only for a little while, and we took again to our mowing. And at last there was nothing left but a small square of grass, standing like a square of linesmen who keep their formation, tall and unbroken, with all the dead lying around them when the battle is over and done.

[20] Belloc continues the narrative; they get on with the mowing.

Can you explain why Belloc uses so many "ands" to join main clauses and sentences?

[21] Then for some little time I rested after all those hours; and the man and I talked together, and a long way off we heard in another field the musical sharpening of a scythe.

[21]–[25] These paragraphs complete the process of mowing the field and bring the day to its close.

(a) *Is the division into five rather short paragraphs justified?*
(b) *Do you feel that any of these might be combined?*

[22] The sunlight slanted powdered and mellow over the breadth of the valley; for day was nearing its end. I went to fetch rakes from the steading; and when I had come back the last of the grass had fallen, and all the field lay flat and smooth, with the very green short grass in lanes between the dead and yellow swathes.

[23] These swathes we raked into cocks to keep them from the dew against our return at daybreak; and we made the cocks as tall and steep as we could, for in that shape they best keep off the dew, and it is easier also to spread them after the sun has risen. Then we raked up every straggling blade, till the whole field was a clean floor for the tedding and the carrying of the

hay next morning. The grass we had mown was but a little over two acres; for that is all the pasture on my little tiny farm.

[24] When we had done all this, there fell upon us the beneficent and deliberate evening; so that as we sat a little while together near the rakes, we saw the valley more solemn and dim around us, and all the trees and hedgerows quite still, and held by a complete silence. Then I paid my companion his wage, and bade him a good night, till we should meet in the same place before sunrise.

[25] He went off with a slow and steady progress, as all our peasants do, making their walking a part of the easy but continual labor of their lives. But I sat on, watching the light creep around towards the north and change, and the waning moon coming up as though by stealth behind the woods of No Man's Land.

[25] Apart from bringing the day to a close, how does the paragraph act as a conclusion to the essay?

COMPOSITION ASSIGNMENT

Write a narrative-descriptive essay in which you describe your return, real or imaginary, to a place with which you have many associations—a summer home, school, camp, any place which will allow you to compare memory with present actuality.

THE GREAT BLIZZARD

Hamlin Garland

Unlike the other two essays of this section, this essay is tightly organized in a chronological order. Its purpose is to describe the beginning, the growth, the climax, the decline, and the aftermath of a blizzard on the plains of Wisconsin. Incidentally, the Lincoln referred to in the essay is Hamlin Garland's brother. Notice that the opening sentence of almost all paragraphs indicates clearly the passage of time.

[1] A blizzard on the prairie corresponds to a storm at sea; it never affects the traveler twice alike. Each Norther seems to have a manner of attack all its own. One storm may be short, sharp, high-keyed, and malevolent, while another approaches slowly, relentlessly, wearing out the souls of its victims by its inexorable and long-continued cold and gloom. One threatens for hours before it comes, the other leaps like a tiger upon the defenseless settlement, catching the children unhoused, the men unprepared; of this character was the first blizzard Lincoln ever saw.

[2] The day was warm and sunny. The eaves dripped musically, and the icicles dropping from the roof fell occasionally with a pleasant crash. The snow grew slushy, and the bells of wood teams jingled merrily all the forenoon as the farmers drove to their timber lands five or six miles away. The schoolroom was uncomfortably warm at times, and the master opened the outside door. It was the eighth day of January. During afternoon recess, as the boys were playing in their shirt sleeves, Lincoln called Milton's attention to a great cloud in the

Intelligent reading and intelligent composition depend upon a student's ability to do his own thinking. Up to this point we have directed this thinking by specific commentary and questions. For this essay, some suggestions in the form of brief headings are given. Using these as an indication of the direction your analysis might take, make a detailed commentary on each paragraph.

[1] Introductory paragraph
Different functions of main clauses

[2] A second introductory paragraph
Purpose of the paragraph
Appeal to the senses

west and north.   A vast, slaty-blue, seamless dome, silent, portentous, with edges of silvery frosty light, was rising.

③ "It's going to storm," said Milton. "It always does when we have a south wind and a cloud like that in the west."

④ When Lincoln set out for home, the sun was still shining, but the edge of the cloud had crept, or more properly slid, across the sun's disk, and its light was growing pale.   Fifteen minutes later the wind from the south ceased— there was a moment of breathless pause, and then, borne on the wings of the north wind, the streaming clouds of soft, large flakes of snow drove in a level line over the homeward-bound scholars, sticking to their clothing and faces and melting rapidly.   It was not yet cold enough to freeze, though the wind was sharper.   It was the growing darkness which troubled Lincoln most.

④ Handling of time sequence Transitions

⑤ By the time he reached home, the wind was a gale, and the snow, a vast blinding cloud, filled the air and hid the road.   Darkness came on almost instantly, and the wind increased in power, as though with the momentum of the snow.   Mr. Stewart came home early, yet the breasts of his horses were already sheathed in snow.   Other teamsters passed, breasting the storm, and calling cheerily to their horses. One team, containing a woman and two men, neighbors living seven miles north, gave up the contest, and turned in at the gate for shelter, confident that they would be able to go on in the morning.   In the barn, while rubbing the ice from the horses, the men joked of their plight and told stories in jovial spirit, saying, "All will be clear by daylight." The boys made merry also, singing songs, popping corn, playing games, in defiance of the storm.

⑤ Atmosphere, mood, related to details

[6] But when they went to bed, at ten o'clock, Lincoln felt a vague premonition of the dread character of the disturbance of nature. It went far beyond any other experience in his short life. The wind howled like ten thousand tigers, and the cold grew more and more intense. The frost seemed to drive in and through the frail tenement; water and food began to freeze within ten feet of the fire.

[6] Key phrase
Relationship of key phrase and supporting details

[7] Lincoln thought that the wind at that hour had attained its upmost fury, but when he awoke in the morning, he perceived how mistaken he had been. He crept to the fire, appalled by the steady, solemn, implacable clamor of the storm. It was like the roarings of all the lions of Africa, the hissing of a wilderness of serpents, the lashing of great trees. It benumbed his thinking, and appalled his heart, beyond any other force he had ever known.

[7] The sense appealed to
Use of simile

[8] The house shook and snapped, the snow beat in muffled, rhythmic pulsations against the walls, or swirled and lashed upon the roof, giving rise to strange, multitudinous, anomalous sounds; now dim and far, now near and all-surrounding; producing an effect of mystery and infinite reach, as though the cabin were a helpless boat, tossing on an angry, limitless sea.

[8] Kind of figure of speech

[9] On looking out, nothing could be seen but the lashing of the wind and snow. When the men attempted to face it, to go to the rescue of the cattle, they found the air impenetrably filled with fine, powdery crystals mixed with the soil caught up from the plowed fields and moving ninety miles an hour. It was impossible to see twenty feet, except at long intervals. Lincoln could not see at all when facing the storm. The instant he stepped into the wind, his face was coated with ice and dirt, as by a

[9] Dominant sensory appeal

dash of mud—a mask which blinded the eyes, and instantly froze to his cheeks. Such was the power of the wind that he could not breathe an instant unprotected. His mouth being once open, it was impossible to draw breath again without turning from the wind.

[10] The day was spent in keeping warm and in feeding the stock at the barn, which Mr. Stewart reached by a desperate dash, during the momentary clearing of the air following some more than usually strong gust. Lincoln attempted to water the horses from the pump, but the wind blew the water out of the pail. So cold had the wind become that a dipperful, thrown into the air, fell as ice. In the house it became more and more difficult to remain cheerful, notwithstanding an abundance of food and fuel.

[10] Same point as paragraph 9
Different method

[11] Oh, that terrible day! Hour after hour they listened to that prodigious, appalling, ferocious uproar. All day Lincoln and Owen moved restlessly to and fro, asking each other, "Won't it ever stop?" To them the storm now seemed too vast, too ungovernable, ever again to be spoken to a calm, even by the Creator Himself. It seemed to Lincoln that no power whatsoever could control such fury; his imagination was unable to conceive of a force greater than this war of wind and snow.

[11], [12] Atmosphere and mood (compare to paragraph 5)

[12] On the third day the family rose with weariness, and looked into each other's faces with horrified surprise. Not even the invincible heart of Duncan Stewart, nor the cheery good nature of his wife, could keep a gloomy silence from settling down upon the house. Conversation was spasmodic, for all were listening anxiously to the invisible furies tearing at the shingles, beating against the door, and shrieking around the eaves. The frost upon

the windows, nearly half an inch thick, thickened into ice, and the room was dim at midday. The fire melted the snow upon the door, and water ran along the floor, while around the keyhole and along every crack, frost formed. The men's faces took on a grim, set look, and the women sat with awed faces and downcast eyes full of unshed tears, their sympathies going out to settlers in new and flimsy cabins.

[13] The men got to the poor dumb animals that day but to water them was impossible. Mr. Stewart went down through the roof of the shed, the doors being completely sealed with solid banks of snow and dirt. One of the guests had a wife and two children left alone in a small cottage six miles farther on, and physical force was necessary to keep him from setting out in face of the deadly tempest. It would have been death to venture out.

[13] Relationship of the two incidents

[14] That night, so disturbed had the entire household become, they lay awake listening, waiting, hoping for a change. About midnight Lincoln noticed that the roar was less steady, and not so high-keyed as before. It lulled at times, and though it returned to the attack with all its former ferocity, there was a perceptible weakening. Its fury was becoming spasmodic. One of the men shouted down to Mr. Stewart, "The storm is over," and when the host called back a ringing word of cheer, Lincoln sank into deep sleep in sheer exhaustion and relief.

[14] Function of paragraph in relationship to essay as a whole

[15] Oh, the joy with which the children melted the ice on the windowpanes, and peered out on the familiar landscape, dazzling, peaceful, under the brilliant sun and wide blue sky! Lincoln looked out over the wide plain, ridged with vast drifts, on the far blue line of timber, on the nearby cottages sending up cheerful columns of

[15] Psychological reaction

smoke (as if to tell him the neighbors were alive), and his heart seemed to fill his throat. But the wind was with him still! So long and so continuously had its voice sounded in his ears, that even in the perfect calm of the moment his imagination supplied its loss with fainter, fancied roarings.

[16] Out in the barn the horses and cattle, hungry and frostbitten, kicked and bellowed in pain, and when the men dug them out, they ran and raced like mad creatures, to start the blood circulating in their numbed and stiffened limbs. The boys helped tunnel to the barn door, cutting through the hard snow as if it were clay. The drifts were solid, and the dirt mixed with the snow was disposed on the surface in beautiful wavelets, like the sands at the bottom of a lake. The drifts would bear a horse, and Duncan's guests were able to go home across lots, riding above the fences, and rattling across over plowed ground.

[16] Description by aftereffects

[17] In the days which followed, grim tales of suffering and heroism were told: tales of the finding of a stagecoach with the driver frozen on his seat and all his passengers within; tales of travelers caught while striving to reach home and families. Cattle had starved in their stalls, and sheep lay buried in heaps beside the fences where they had crowded together to keep warm. Lincoln had gained a new conception of the prairie. However bright and beautiful it might be in summer under skies of June, it could be terrible when the Norther was abroad in his wrath. It now seemed as pitiless and as destructive as the polar ocean. Nothing could live there unhoused. All was at the mercy of the North Wind, whom only the Lord Sun could tame.

[17], [18] As with introduction, two conclusions
   Function
   Difference

18   This was the worst storm of the winter, though the wind seemed never to sleep. To and fro, from north to south and south to north, the dry snow sifted till it was like fine sand that rolled under the heel with a ringing sound on cold days. After each storm the restless wind got to work to pile the new-fallen flakes into ridges behind every fence or bush, filling every ravine and forcing the teamsters into the fields and out upon the open lands. It was a savage and gloomy time for the boys, with only the pleasure of their school to break the monotony of cold.

COMPOSITION ASSIGNMENT

Write a narrative-descriptive essay of an event which has growth and climax. One possibility is a natural event such as a storm, flood, or fire. Another is a public spectacle such as a rodeo, circus, political convention.

From OLD TIMES ON THE MISSISSIPPI

Mark Twain

This selection consists of the first two chapters of *Old Times on the Mississippi*, which Samuel Clemens (Mark Twain) published in 1875, some dozen years after the life which the book portrays had come to an end because of the decline of the river trade during the Civil War. The original work contains his happy, nostalgic recollections of the great days of his youth and the river. Later, in 1883, he expanded the book to include chapters in which he sadly describes the scene as it appeared when he returned to it in its days of decline.

The chapters included here cannot be described as primarily narrative or primarily descriptive. They include descriptions, character sketches, and anecdotes. Mark Twain combines these materials to give us at once an account of a phase of his life and a picture of a time, a place, a way of life in the nation's history. Thus, although the medium is that of the personal reminiscence, the interest is as much historical as autobiographical.

The Boy's Ambition

[1] When I was a boy there was but one permanent ambition among my comrades in our village* on the west bank of the Mississippi River. That was, to be a steamboatman. We had transient ambitions of other sorts but they were only transient. When a circus came and went, it left us all burning to become clowns; the first Negro minstrel show that ever came to our section left us all suffering to try that kind

[1] This paragraph is developed by contrast and example.

What are the key words of the contrast?

---

* *Village:* Hannibal, Missouri.

of life; now and then we had a hope that, if we lived and were good, God would permit us to be pirates. These ambitions faded out, each in its turn; but the ambition to be a steamboatman always remained.

2 Once a day a cheap, gaudy packet arrived upward from St. Louis, and another downward from Keokuk. Before these events, the day was glorious with expectancy; after they had transpired, the day was a dead and empty thing. Not only the boys, but the whole village, felt this. After all these years I can picture that old time to myself now, just as it was then: the white town drowsing in the sunshine of a summer's morning; the streets empty or pretty nearly so; one or two clerks sitting in front of the Water Street stores, with their splint-bottomed chairs tilted back against the wall, chins on breasts, hats slouched over their faces, asleep—with shingle-shavings enough around to show what broke them down; a sow and a litter of pigs loafing along the sidewalk, doing a good business in watermelon rinds and seeds; two or three lonely little freight piles scattered about the "levee"; a pile of "skids" on the slope of the stone-paved wharf, and the fragrant town drunkard asleep in the shadow of them; two or three wood flats at the head of the wharf but nobody to listen to the peaceful lapping of the wavelets against them; the great Mississippi, the majestic, the magnificent Mississippi, rolling its mile-wide tide along, shining in the sun; the dense forest away on the other side; the "point" above the town, and the "point" below, bounding the river-glimpse and turning it into a sort of sea, and withal a very still and brilliant and lonely one. Presently a film of dark smoke appears above one of those remote "points"; instantly a Negro drayman, famous for his quick eye and prodigious voice, lifts up the cry, "S-t-e-a-m-boat a-comin'!" and the scene changes! The town drunkard stirs, the clerks

2 Although this paragraph follows a chronological order in recounting the events of a day, it is descriptive rather than narrative. It does not tell the story of a particular day, but recounts typical events of a typical day in order to give an impression of the routine life of a riverside village. Note the close relationship between sentence 2 and the last sentence; respectively, they foreshadow and summarize the **cyclical** nature of the sequence of events which provides the basic form of the paragraph. Thus the structure of the paragraph reflects and emphasizes the point that, after the brief exhilaration over the steamer's calls, the town reverts to its former deadness.

In sentence 4, note that the details are introduced by a clear statement of the **retrospective** point of view; we are informed that we are reading recollections rather than immediate observations, and we can expect that the author's memories will be heightened by his **nostalgic** mood. Observe throughout your study of the selection the interdependence of tone and point of view.

Twain states that the packet was "cheap" and "gaudy." However, the picture he paints may seem to contradict this judgment.

(a) *List the phrases which seem to contradict the judgment.*
(b) *How do you explain the seeming contradiction?*
(c) *How does "husbanded grandeur" fit into this contradiction?*
(d) *What is the difference between the tone of "gorgeous" as applied to the paddle boxes and of "magnificent" as applied to the Mississippi?*

wake up, a furious clatter of drays follows, every house and store pours out a human contribution, and all in a twinkling the dead town is alive and moving. Drays, carts, men, boys, all go hurrying from many quarters to a common center, the wharf. Assembled there, the people fasten their eyes upon the coming boat as upon a wonder they are seeing for the first time. And the boat *is* rather a handsome sight, too. She is long and sharp and trim and pretty; she has two tall, fancy-topped chimneys, with a gilded device of some kind swung between them; a fanciful pilothouse, all glass and "gingerbread," perched on top of the "texas" deck behind them, the paddle-boxes are gorgeous with a picture or with the gilded rays above the boat's name; the boiler deck, the hurricane deck, and the texas deck are fenced and ornamented with clean white railings; there is a flag gallantly flying from the jack staff; the furnace doors are open and the fires glaring bravely; the upper decks are black with passengers; the captain stands by the big bell, calm, imposing, the envy of all; great volumes of the blackest smoke are rolling and tumbling out of the chimneys—a husbanded grandeur created with a bit of pitch-pine just before arriving at a town; the crew are grouped on the forecastle; the broad stage is run far out over the port bow and an envied deck-hand stands picturesquely on the end of it with a coil of rope in his hand; the pent steam is screaming though the gauge-cocks: the captain lifts his hand, a bell rings, the wheels stop; then they turn back, churning the water to foam, and the steamer is at rest. Then such a scramble as there is to get aboard and to get ashore, and to take in freight and to discharge freight, all at once and the same time; and such a yelling and cursing as the mates facilitate it all with! Ten minutes later the steamer is under way again, with no flag on the jack-staff and no black smoke issuing from the chimneys. After

Another interesting feature of the paragraph is the structure of the sentences in relation to the structure of the paragraph as a whole. The fourth sentence is an exceptionally long one, consisting of an extensive list of details signalled by the colon that follows the introductory statement. Yet it is a unified and coherent sentence because the details are presented in **parallel** form; that is, each follows essentially the same grammatical construction.

(**e**) *What is this grammatical construction?*

Moreover, the details are arranged within the sentence according to a plan; instead of being caught up in a digression, we are led toward the event that is central to the paragraph.

(**f**) *Explain this plan.*
(**g**) *What would be the effect upon the paragraph if the compact parallelism of sentence 4 were replaced by several sentences of varied construction?*

Sentence 10, describing the steamboat, is another extremely long one; it consists of numerous main clauses, each of which might be a separate sentence. Mark Twain's combining them into one has again served to create a sub-unit within the long paragraph.

The length of paragraph 2 raises a question that often troubles students: how long or how complex should a paragraph be? No rule can be given, but it is helpful to remember that paragraphs are a means of subdividing a whole. If Mark Twain had intended what is now a paragraph to be a self-sufficient sketch, he might well have subdivided it. However, as it stands, it has unity as a subtopic of a more general topic identified by the chapter heading.

(**h**) *At what points might the paragraph be divided?*

ten more minutes the town is dead again, and the town drunkard asleep by the skids once more.

3 My father was a justice of the peace and I supposed he possessed the power of life and death over all men and could hang anybody that offended him. This was distinction enough for me as a general thing, but the desire to be a steamboatman kept intruding, nevertheless. I first wanted to be a cabin-boy, so that I could come out with a white apron on and shake a table-cloth over the side, where all my old comrades could see me; later I thought I would rather be the deck-hand who stood on the end of the stage-plank with the coil of rope in his hand, because he was particularly conspicuous. But these were only day-dreams—they were too heavenly to be contemplated as real possibilities. By and by one of our boys went away. He was not heard of for a long time. At last he turned up as apprentice engineer or "striker" on a steamboat. This thing shook the bottom out of all my Sunday-school teachings. That boy had been notoriously worldly and I was just the reverse; yet he was exalted to this eminence and I left in obscurity and misery. There was nothing generous about this fellow in his greatness. He would always manage to have a rusty bolt to scrub while his boat tarried at our town, and he would sit on the inside guard and scrub it, where we all could see him and envy him and loathe him. And whenever his boat was laid up he would come home and swell around the town in his blackest and greasiest clothes, so that nobody could help remembering that he was a steamboatman; and he used all sorts of steamboat technicalities in his talk, as if he were so used to them that he forgot common people could not understand them. He would speak of the "labboard" side of a horse in an easy, natural way that would

COMPOSITION ASSIGNMENT

Write a descriptive paragraph developed chronologically. Choose a subject which changes in aspect with the passage of time. It will be helpful to choose a distinct period of time—a day, a season, or a year. Keep in mind the possibility of such a cyclical development as Mark Twain has used in paragraph 2.

3 Again we have an extremely long paragraph to which the remarks made above are applicable.

(a) *What is the topic idea of the paragraph?*
(b) *Identify the three stages in the development of the idea. What is the topic of each section?*
(c) *Trace the shift in tone from section to section. How does the point of view govern the tone of the last section?*
(d) *What is the effect of "admired and hated"? (Compare this to the comment on paragraph 19, page 34.) There are many other interesting turns of phrase. List several and be prepared to explain what they contribute to the paragraph.*

make one wish he was dead. And he was always talking about "St. Looy" like an old citizen; he would refer casually to occasions when he "was coming down Fourth Street," or when he was "passing by the Planter's House," or when there was a fire and he took a turn on the brakes of "the old Big Missouri"; and then he would go on and lie about how many towns the size of ours were burned down there that day. Two or three of the boys had long been persons of consideration among us because they had been to St. Louis once and had a vague general knowledge of its wonders, but the day of their glory was over now. They lapsed into a humble silence and learned to disappear when the ruthless "cub" engineer approached. This fellow had money, too, and hair oil. Also an ignorant silver watch and a showy brass watch-chain. He wore a leather belt and used no suspenders. If ever a youth was cordially admired and hated by his comrades, this one was. No girl could withstand his charms. He "cut out" every boy in the village. When his boat blew up at last, it diffused a tranquil contentment among us such as we had not known for months. But when he came home the next week, alive, renowned, and appeared in church all battered up and bandaged, a shining hero, stared at and wondered over by everybody, it seemed to us that the partiality of Providence for an undeserving reptile had reached a point where it was open to criticism.

[4] This creature's career could produce but one result, and it speedily followed. Boy after boy managed to get on the river. The minister's son became an engineer. The doctor's and postmaster's sons became "mud clerks"; the wholesale liquor dealer's son became a barkeeper on a boat; four sons of the chief merchant and two sons of the county judge became pilots. Pilot was the grandest position of all.

The pilot, even in those days of trivial wages, had a princely salary—from a hundred and fifty to two hundred and fifty dollars a month, and no board to pay. Two months of his wages would pay a preacher's salary for a year. Now some of us were left disconsolate. We could not get on the river—at least our parents would not let us.

5 So by and by I ran away. I said I would never come home again till I was a pilot and could come in glory. But somehow I could not manage it. I went meekly aboard a few of the boats that lay packed together like sardines at the long St. Louis wharf, and humbly inquired for the pilots, but got only a cold shoulder and short words from mates and clerks. I had to make the best of this sort of treatment for the time being, but I had comforting daydreams of a future when I should be a great and honored pilot, with plenty of money, and could kill some of these mates and clerks and pay for them.

6 Months afterward the hope within me struggled to a reluctant death, and I found myself without an ambition. But I was ashamed to go home. I was in Cincinnati, and I set to work to map out a new career. I had been reading about the recent exploration of the river Amazon by an expedition sent out by our government. It was said that the expedition, owing to difficulties, had not thoroughly explored a part of the country lying about the headwaters, some four thousand miles from the mouth of the river. It was only fifteen hundred miles from Cincinnati to New Orleans, where I could doubtless get a ship. I had thirty dollars left; I would go and complete the exploration of the Amazon. This was all the thought I gave to the subject. I never was great in matters of detail. I packed my valise, and took passage on an ancient tub called the *Paul Jones*, for New Orleans. For the sum of sixteen dollars, I

5 - 14 These paragraphs show the interplay of two points of view, which is often characteristic of retrospective writing. Since human beings develop and change, there are two persons to consider here—the young Samuel Clemens, would-be pilot, and the older Mark Twain, ex-pilot and writer looking back on his youth. As you read, pay careful attention to the tone; observe not only the youth's attitudes but also the attitude of the mature writer. Jot down phrases that help reveal both attitudes.

had the scarred and tarnished splendors of "her" main saloon principally to myself, for she was not a creature to attract the eye of wiser travelers.

⑦ When we presently got under way and went poking down the broad Ohio, I became a new being and the subject of my own admiration. I was a traveler! A word never had tasted so good in my mouth before. I had an exultant sense of being bound for mysterious lands and distant climes which I never have felt in so uplifting a degree since. I was in such a glorified condition that all ignoble feelings departed out of me, and I was able to look down and pity the untraveled with a compassion that had hardly a trace of contempt in it. Still, when we stopped at villages and woodyards, I could not help lolling carelessly upon the railings of the boiler deck to enjoy the envy of the country boys on the bank. If they did not seem to discover me, I presently sneezed to attract their attention, or moved to a position where they could not help seeing me. And as soon as I knew they saw me I gaped and stretched, and gave other signs of being mightily bored with traveling.

⑧ I kept my hat off all the time, and stayed where the wind and the sun could strike me, because I wanted to get the bronzed and weather-beaten look of an old traveler. Before the second day was half gone I experienced a joy which filled me with the purest gratitude, for I saw that the skin had begun to blister and peel off my face and neck. I wished that the boys and girls at home could see me now.

⑧ *Can you identify any feelings that you have had at any time with the youth's feelings recorded here?*

⑨ We reached Louisville in time—at least the neighborhood of it. We stuck hard and fast on the rocks in the middle of the river and lay there four days. I was now beginning to feel a strong sense of being a part of the boat's family, a sort of infant son to the captain and younger brother to the officers. There is no estimating the pride I took in this grandeur or the affection that began to swell and grow in me for those people. I could not know how the lordly steamboatman scorns that sort of presumption in a mere landsman. I particularly longed to acquire the least trifle of notice from the big stormy mate, and I was on the alert for an opportunity to do him a service to that end. It came at last. The riotous pow-wow of setting a spar was going on down on the forecastle and I went down there and stood around in the way—or mostly skipping out of it—till the mate suddenly roared a general order for somebody to bring him a capstan bar. I sprang to his side and said: "Tell me where it is—I'll fetch it!"

[10] If a ragpicker had offered to do a diplomatic service for the Emperor of Russia, the monarch could not have been more astounded than the mate was. He even stopped swearing. He stood and stared down at me. It took him ten seconds to scrape his disjointed remains together again. Then he said impressively: "Well, if this don't beat hell!" and turned to his work with the air of a man who had been confronted with a problem too abstruse for solution.

[11] I crept away and courted solitude for the rest of the day. I did not go to dinner, I stayed away from supper until everybody else had finished. I did not feel so much like a member of the boat's family now as before. However, my spirits returned, in installments, as we pursued our way down the river. I was sorry I hated the mate so, because it was not in (young) human nature not to admire him. He was huge and muscular, his face was bearded and whiskered all over, he had a red woman and a blue woman tattooed on his right arm—one on each side of a blue anchor with a red rope to it—and

in the matter of profanity he was perfect. When he was getting out cargo at a landing, I was always where I could see and hear. He felt all the majesty of his great position and made the world feel it too. When he gave even the simplest order, he discharged it like a blast of lightning and sent a long, reverberating peal of profanity thundering after it. I could not help contrasting the way in which the average landsman would give an order with the mate's way of doing it. If the landsman should wish the gang-plank moved a foot farther forward, he would probably say, "James, or William, one of you push that plank forward, please;" but put the mate in his place, and he would roar out, "Here, now, start that gang-plank for'ard! Lively, now! What're you about! Snatch it! *snatch* it! There! there! aft again! Don't you hear me? Dash it to dash! are you going to *sleep* over it! '*Vast* heaving. 'Vast heaving, I tell you! Going to heave it clear astern? WHERE're you going with that barrel! *for'ard* with it 'fore I make you swallow it, you dash-dash-dash-*dashed* split between a tired mud-turtle and a crippled hearse-horse!"

[12]   I wished I could talk like that.

[13]   When the soreness of my adventure with the mate had somewhat worn off, I began timidly to make up to the humblest official connected with the boat—the night watchman. He snubbed my advances at first, but I presently ventured to offer him a new chalk pipe, and that softened him. So he allowed me to sit with him by the big bell on the hurricane-deck, and in time he melted into conversation. He could not well have helped it, I hung with such homage on his words and so plainly showed that I felt honored by his notice. He told me the names of dim capes and shadowy islands as we glided by them in the solemnity of the night,

[13], [14]   Here the interplay of the two points of view shows very clearly. The sixth sentence contains a deliberate self-correction; the author is pointing out the difference between his present view and his youthful attitude. In these paragraphs the author conveys directly both the worshipful wonder of the youngster and a more mature awareness ("incredible adventures") of the absurdity of his trust. Observe that he also suggests the youth's gullibility indirectly through the details of the watchman's "plaintive history" (paragraph 13, sentences 10–13).

under the winking stars, and by and by got to talking about himself. He seemed over-sentimental for a man whose salary was six dollars a week—or rather he might have seemed so to an older person than I. But I drank in his words hungrily, and with a faith that might have moved mountains if it had been applied judiciously. What was it to me that he was soiled and seedy and fragrant with gin? What was it to me that his grammar was bad, his construction worse, and his profanity so void of art that it was an element of weakness rather than strength in his conversation? He was a wronged man, a man who had seen trouble, and that was enough for me. As he mellowed into his plaintive history his tears dripped upon the lantern in his lap, and I cried too from sympathy. He said he was the son of an English nobleman—either an earl or an alderman, he could not remember which, but believed was both; his father, the nobleman, loved him but his mother hated him from the cradle; and so while he was still a little boy he was sent to "one of them old, ancient colleges,"—he couldn't remember which; and by and by his father died and his mother seized the property and "shook" him, as he phrased it. After his mother shook him, members of the nobility with whom he was acquainted used their influence to get him the position of "lob-lolly-boy in a ship;" and from that point my watchman threw off all trammels of date and locality and branched out into a narrative that bristled all along with incredible adventures; a narrative that was so reeking with bloodshed and so crammed with hairbreadth escapes and the most engaging and unconscious personal villainies, that I sat speechless, enjoying, shuddering, wondering, worshiping.

[14] It was a sore blight to find out afterward that he was a low, vulgar, ignorant, senti-

Here a **transparency** is created. The details are so absurd that, even though they are reported straightforwardly, we see through the youth's acceptance of them and understand that the author is presenting the watchman as an old fraud and his younger self as naively credulous. The effect is so clear that we do not really need the disclosure of paragraph 14.

mental, half-witted humbug, an untraveled native of the wilds of Illinois, who had absorbed wildcat literature and appropriated its marvels, until in time he had woven odds and ends of the mess into this yarn, and then gone on telling it to fledglings like me, until he had come to believe it himself.

Learning the River

[15] What with lying on the rocks four days at Louisville, and some other delays, the poor old *Paul Jones* fooled away about two weeks in making the voyage from Cincinnati to New Orleans. This gave me a chance to get acquainted with one of the pilots, and he taught me how to steer the boat, and thus made the fascination of river life more potent than ever for me.

[16] It also gave me a chance to get acquainted with a youth who had taken deck passage— more's the pity, for he easily borrowed six dollars of me on a promise to return to the boat and pay it back to me that day after we should arrive. But he probably died or forgot, for he never came. It was doubtless the former, since he had said his parents were wealthy, and he only traveled deck passage because it was cooler.

[16] Here is a paragraph in which the mature point of view is communicated entirely indirectly, again through transparency. Although the last two sentences are offered in the guise of straightforward explanation, as if from the point of view of the author, the reader has no difficulty in recognizing that the explanation is a joke at the expense of his younger self. Such a transparency results from a kind of verbal irony (see the comments to

[17]   I soon discovered two things.   One was that a vessel would not be likely to sail for the mouth of the Amazon under ten or twelve years, and the other was that the nine or ten dollars still left in my pocket would not suffice for so impossible an exploration as I had planned, even if I could afford to wait for a ship.   Therefore it followed that I must contrive a new career.   The *Paul Jones* was now bound for St. Louis.   I planned a siege against my pilot, and at the end of three hard days he surrendered. He agreed to teach me the Mississippi River from New Orleans to St. Louis for five hundred dollars, payable out of the first wages I should receive after graduating.   I entered upon the small enterprise of "learning" twelve or thirteen hundred miles of the great Mississippi River with the easy confidence of my time of life.   If I had really known what I was about to require of my faculties, I should not have had the courage to begin.   I supposed that all a pilot had to do was to keep his boat in the river, and I did not consider that that could be much of a trick, since it was so wide.

[18]   The boat backed out from New Orleans at four in the afternoon, and it was "our watch" until eight.   Mr. Bixby, my chief, "straightened her up," plowed her along past the sterns of the other boats that lay at the Levee, and then said, "here, take her; shave those steamships as close as you'd peel an apple."   I took the wheel and my heart went down into my boots; for it seemed to me that we were about to scrape the side off every ship in the line, we were so close. I held my breath and began to claw the boat away from the danger; and I had my own opinion of the pilot who had known no better than to get us into such peril, but I was too wise to express it.   In half a minute I had a wide margin of safety intervening between the *Paul Jones* and the ships, and within ten seconds more

paragraph 4, page 19). The details of the explanation "said his parents were wealthy" and "deck passage because it was cooler" are such that reader rejects them on the ground of his experience of the world and sees that the author is dissociating himself from the stated interpretation. Thus we have a discrepancy, the basis of irony in all its forms. (See also Summary, page 25.) As you continue reading the chapter, watch for other examples of the effect.

[17], [18]   Consider whether we can believe that the views which Mark Twain attributes to his younger self were actually as represented by "small enterprise" (sentence 6 of paragraph 17 and the last sentences of paragraphs 17 and 18).

If these thoughts are the product of the adult Mark Twain's humorous imagination rather than the actual thoughts of the youth, do they exist merely for the sake of a joke, or are they a means of emphasizing a quality that Mark Twain is consistently developing as characteristic of his youth?

I was set aside in disgrace and Mr. Bixby was going into danger again and flaying me alive with abuse of my cowardice. I was stung, but I was obliged to admire the easy confidence with which my chief loafed from side to side of his wheel and trimmed the ships so closely that disaster seemed ceaselessly imminent. When he had cooled a little he told me that the easy water was close ashore and the current outside, and therefore we must hug the bank, up-stream, to get the benefit of the former, and stay well out, down-stream, to take advantage of the latter. In my own mind I resolved to be a down-stream pilot and leave the up-streaming to people dead to prudence.

20 Now and then Mr. Bixby called my attention to certain things. Said he, "This is Six-Mile Point." I assented. It was pleasant enough information but I could not see the bearing of it. I was not conscious that it was a matter of any interest to me. Another time he said, "This is Nine-Mile Point." Later he said, "This is Twelve-Mile Point." They were all about level with the water's edge; they all looked about alike to me; they were monotonously unpicturesque. I hoped Mr. Bixby would change the subject. But no, he would crowd up around a point, hugging the shore with affection, and then say: "The slack water ends here, abreast this bunch of China trees; now we cross over." So he crossed over. He gave me the wheel once or twice but I had no luck. I either came near chipping off the edge of a sugar planation, or else I yawed too far from shore, and so I dropped back into disgrace again and got abused.

20 The watch was ended at last, and we took supper and went to bed. At midnight the glare of a lantern shone in my eyes, and the night watchman said:

19 *Point out an instance in this paragraph of the tone discussed in the comments above.*

COMPOSITION ASSIGNMENT

Try an exercise in creating a transparency. Writing in the first person, tell an anecdote at your own expense. Try to show your view at the time the episode occurred without telling the reader directly (for example refer to paragraphs 13 and 16). Your reader should understand as he follows the account—not merely at the end—that the attitude you held at the time of the episode you now consider erroneous. You can, for example, show gullibility, false pride, needless fear, or embarrassment.

[21]   "Come! turn out!"

[22]   And then he left. I could not understand this extraordinary procedure; so I presently gave up trying to, and dozed off to sleep. Pretty soon the watchman was back again, and this time he was gruff. I was annoyed. I said:

[23]   "What do you want to come bothering around here in the middle of the night for? Now, as like as not, I'll not get to sleep again to-night."

[24]   The watchman said:—

[25]   "Well, if this an't good, I'm blessed."

[26]   The "off-watch" was just turning in and I heard some brutal laughter from them, and such remarks as "Hello watchman! an't the new cub turned out yet? He's delicate, likely. Give him some sugar in a rag and send for the chambermaid to sing rock-a-by baby to him."

[27]   About this time Mr. Bixby appeared on the scene. Something like a minute later I was climbing the pilot-house steps with some of my clothes on and the rest in my arms. Mr. Bixby was close behind, commenting. Here was something fresh—this thing of getting up in the middle of the night to go to work. It was a detail in piloting that had never occurred to me at all. I knew that boats ran all night, but somehow I had never happened to reflect that somebody had to get up out of a warm bed to run them. I began to fear that piloting was not quite so romantic as I had imagined it was; there was something very real and work-like about this new phase of it.

[27]   Observe that what occurs in the minute between Mr. Bixby's appearance and the cub's hasty ascent to the pilot house is deliberately left to the reader's imagination, though Mark Twain does not resort to the trite device of saying something to the effect of "What followed Mr. Bixby's appearance can safely be left to the reader." The author's handling of the episode encourages the reader's participation and also produces an agreeable change of pace and emphasis in contrasting with fully detailed, probably exaggerated development of such passages as the portrait of the mate (paragraph 11, pages 78–79).

"Commenting" in sentence 2 is purposeful **understatement,** *in keeping with the underplaying of this episode. What does the word mean?*

28 It was a rather dingy night, although a fair number of stars were out. The big mate was at the wheel and he had the old tub pointed at a star and was holding her straight up the middle of the river. The shores on either hand were not much more than half a mile apart, but they seemed wonderfully far away and ever so vague and indistinct. The mate said:

"We've got to land at Jones's plantation, sir."

The vengeful spirit in me exulted. I said to myself, "I wish you joy of your job, Mr. Bixby; you'll have a good time finding Mr. Jones's plantation such a night as this, and I hope you never *will* find it as long as you live."

Mr. Bixby said to the mate:

"Upper end of the plantation, or the lower?"

"Upper."

"I can't do it. The stumps are out of water at this stage. It's no great distance to the lower, and you'll have to get along with that."

"All right, sir. If Jones don't like it he'll have to lump it, I reckon."

And then the mate left. My exultation began to cool and my wonder to come up. Here was a man who not only proposed to find this plantation on such a night, but to find either end of it you preferred. I dreadfully wanted to ask a question, but I was carrying about as many short answers as my cargo-room would admit of, so I held my peace. All I desired to ask Mr. Bixby was the simple question whether he was ass enough to really imagine he was going to find that plantation on a night when all plantations were exactly alike and all of the same color. But I held in. I used to have fine inspirations of prudence in those days.

Mr. Bixby made for the shore and soon was scraping it, just the same as if it had been daylight. And not only that but singing:

Father in heaven, the day is declining, etc.

28 Here begins the first of two extensively developed episodes of the chapter. For the remainder of the chapter, the numerous paragraphs that result from the standard practice of changing paragraphs with every change of speaker are left unnumbered. Instead, the numbers are used to indicate the principle sections only.

In this section you should observe the continued emphasis on the cub's cocky skepticism, which seems to have been modified only in that it is no longer expressed aloud, in contrast with the mature writer's evident appreciation of Mr. Bixby's skill.

It seemed to me that I had put my life in the keeping of a peculiarly reckless outcast. Presently he turned on me and said:—

"What's the name of the first point above New Orleans?"

I was gratified to be able to answer promptly, and I did. I said I didn't know.

"Don't *know*?"

This manner jolted me. I was down at the foot again, in a moment. But I had to say just what I had said before.

"Well, you're a smart one!" said Mr. Bixby. "What's the name of the *next* point?"

Once more I didn't know.

"Well, this beats anything. Tell me the name of *any* point or place I told you."

I studied awhile and decided that I couldn't.

"Look-a-here! What do you start out from, above Twelve Mile Point, to cross over?"

"I—I—don't know."

"You—you—don't know?" mimicking my drawling manner of speech. "What *do* you know?"

"I—I—nothing, for certain."

"By the great Caesar's ghost I believe you! You're the stupidest dunderhead I ever saw or ever heard of, so help me Moses! The idea of *you* being a pilot—*you*! Why, you don't know enough to pilot a cow down a lane."

Oh, but his wrath was up! He was a nervous man, and he shuffled from one side of his wheel to the other as if the floor was hot. He would boil awhile to himself, and then overflow and scald me again.

"Look-a-here! What do you suppose I told you the names of those points for?"

I tremblingly considered a moment and then the devil of temptation provoked me to say:

"Well to—to—be entertaining, I thought."

This was a red rag to the bull. He raged and stormed so (he was crossing river at the time) that I judged it made him blind, because he

Contrast the style in which the author presents Mr. Bixby's reaction to the cub's ignorance with the use of understatement pointed out on page 84.

What devices are employed?

86

ran over the steering oar of a trading scow. Of course the traders sent up a volley of red-hot profanity. Never was a man so grateful as Mr. Bixby was: because he was brimful and here were subjects who could *talk back*. He threw open a window, thrust his head out, and such an irruption followed as I never had heard before. The fainter and farther away the scow-men's curses drifted, the higher Mr. Bixby lifted his voice and the weightier his adjectives grew. When he closed the window he was empty. You could have drawn a seine through his system and not caught curses enough to disturb your mother with. Presently he said to me in the gentlest way:—

"My boy, you must get a little memorandum-book, and every time I tell you a thing, put it down right away. There's only one way to be a pilot and that is to get this entire river by heart. You have to know it just like A B C."

That was a dismal revelation to me; for my memory was never loaded with anything but blank cartridges. However, I did not feel discouraged long. I judged that it was best to make some allowances, for doubtless Mr. Bixby was "stretching." Presently he pulled a rope and struck a few strokes on the big bell. The stars were all gone, now, and the night was as black as ink. I could hear the wheels churn along the bank, but I was not entirely certain that I could see the shore. The voice of the invisible watchman called up from the hurricane deck:

"What's this, sir?"

"Jones's plantation."

I said to myself, I wish I might venture to offer a small bet that it isn't. But I did not chirp. I only waited to see. Mr. Bixby handled the engine-bells, and in due time the boat's nose came to the land, a torch glowed from the forecastle, a man skipped ashore, a voice on the bank said: "Gimme de carpet-bag, Mars' Jones," and the next moment we were standing up the river again, all serene. I reflected deeply awhile, and then said—but not aloud—Well, the finding of that plantation was the luckiest accident that ever happened, but it couldn't happen again in a hundred years. And I fully believed it *was* an accident, too.

[29] By the time we had gone seven or eight hundred miles up the river, I had learned to be a tolerably plucky up-stream steersman, in daylight, and before we reached St. Louis I had made a trifle of progress in night-work, but only a trifle. I had a note-book that fairly bristled with the names of towns, "points," bars, islands, bends, reaches, etc.; but the information was to be found only in the note-book—none of it was in my head. It made my heart ache to think I had only got half of the river set down; for as our watch was four hours off and four hours on, day and night, there was a long four-hour gap in my book for every time I had slept since the voyage began.

[30] My chief was presently hired to go on a big New Orleans boat, and I packed my satchel and went with him. She was a grand affair. When I stood in her pilot-house I was so far above the water that I seemed perched on a mountain; and her decks stretched so far away, fore and aft, below me, that I wondered how I could ever have considered the little *Paul Jones* a large craft. There were other differences too. The *Paul Jones's* pilot-house was a cheap, dingy, battered rattle-trap, cramped for room: but here was a sumptuous glass temple; room enough to have a dance in, showy red and gold window-curtains; an imposing sofa; leather cushions and a back to the high bench where visiting pilots sit to spin yarns and "look at the river"; bright, fanciful "cuspidores" instead of

Compare the reaction of the cub to Mr. Bixby's success at Jones's landing with the reaction of the narrator of "The Master" to his discovery of the young shipmaster's competence (pages 24–25).

What implied comment is Mark Twain making about the cub's development up to this point?

[29] Paragraphs 29 and 30 make a transition between the two major episodes concerning Mr. Bixby. Paragraph 29 accounts for the passage of time and suggests that the cub has accumulated some practical experience.

Does it also suggest a change in attitude?

[30] After accounting for the change of scene, this paragraph offers an extensive description of a "big New Orleans boat." Again the question of point of view is worth considering. Consider the effect of "sumptuous," "imposing," and "costly with inlaid work" in the early part of the paragraph.

(a) *Is Mark Twain describing the steamboat as it appears in his memory or recording the impression made on a young man of limited experience?*
(b) *What other words and phrases are similar in tone to those listed above?*

a broad wooden box filled with sawdust; nice
new oilcloth on the floor; a hospitable big stove
for winter; a wheel as high as my head costly
with inlaid work; a wire tiller-rope; bright
brass knobs for the bells; and a tidy, white-
aproned, black "texas-tender," to bring up
tarts and ices and coffee during mid-watch,
day and night. Now this was "something like";
and so I began to take heart once more to
believe that piloting was a romantic sort of
occupation after all. The moment we were
under way I began to prowl about the great
steamer and fill myself with joy. She was as
clean and as dainty as a drawing-room; when
I looked down her long, gilded saloon, it was
like gazing through a splendid tunnel; she had
an oil-picture, by some gifted sign-painter, on
every stateroom door; she glittered with no
end of prism-fringed chandeliers; the clerk's
office was elegant, the bar was marvelous, and
the barkeeper had been barbered and up-
holstered at incredible cost. The boiler-deck
(*i.e.*, the second story of the boat, so to speak)
was as spacious as a church, it seemed to me; so
with the forecastle; and there was no pitiful
handful of deck-hands, firemen, and roust-
abouts down there, but a whole battalion of
men. The fires were fiercely glaring from a
long row of furnaces, and over them were eight
huge boilers! This was unutterable pomp.
The mighty engines—but enough of this. I
had never felt so fine before. And when I found
that the regiment of natty servants respectfully
"sir'd" me, my satisfaction was complete.

31   When I returned to the pilot-house St.
Louis was gone and I was lost. Here was a
piece of river which was all down in my book
but I could make neither head nor tail of it:
you understand, it was turned around. I had
seen it, when coming up-stream, but I had
never faced about to see how it looked when it

31 (a) *How does the opening paragraph
of this section resemble paragraph 29?*
(b) *What is the value of the resemblance
in the development of the chapter?*

This section recounts another
demonstration of the pilot's skill. As
you read it, ask yourself in what ways

was behind me. My heart broke again, for it was plain that I had got to learn this troublesome river *both ways.*

The pilot-house was full of pilots, going down to "look at the river." What is called the "upper river" (the two hundred miles between St. Louis and Cairo, where the Ohio comes in) was low; and the Mississippi changes its channel so constantly that the pilots used to always find it necessary to run down to Cairo to take a fresh look, when their boats were to lie in port a week, that is, when the water was at a low stage. A deal of this "looking at the river" was done by poor fellows who seldom had a berth, and whose only hope of getting one lay in their being always freshly posted and therefore ready to drop into the shoes of some reputable pilot, for a single trip, on account of such pilot's sudden illness, or some other necessity. And a good many of them constantly ran up and down inspecting the river, not because they ever really hoped to get a berth but because (they being guests of the boat) it was cheaper to "look at the river" than stay ashore and pay board. In time these fellows grew dainty in their tastes, and only infested boats that had an established reputation for setting good tables. All visiting pilots were useful, for they were always ready and willing, winter or summer, night or day, to go out in the yawl and help buoy the channel or assist the boat's pilots in any way they could. They were likewise welcomed because all pilots are tireless talkers, when gathered together, and as they talk only about the river they are always understood and are always interesting. Your true pilot cares nothing about anything on earth but the river, and his pride in his occupation surpasses the pride of kings.

We had a fine company of these river inspectors along, this trip. There were eight or ten; and there was abundance of room for them in our great pilot-house. Two or three of them

it differs from the episode of section 28 and what the differences contribute to the development of the selection.

wore polished silk hats, elaborate shirt-fronts, diamond breastpins, kid gloves, and patent-leather boots. They were choice in their English, and bore themselves with a dignity proper to men of solid means and prodigious reputation as pilots. The others were more or less loosely clad, and wore upon their heads tall felt cones that were suggestive of the days of the Commonwealth.

I was a cipher in this august company, and felt subdued, not to say torpid. I was not even of sufficient consequence to assist at the wheel when it was necessary to put the tiller hard down in a hurry; the guest that stood nearest did that when occasion required—and this was pretty much all the time, because of the crookedness of the channel and the scant water. I stood in a corner; and the talk I listened to took the hope all out of me. One visitor said to another:—

"Jim, how did you run Plum Point, coming up?"

"It was in the night, there, and I ran it the way one of the boys on the *Diana* told me; started out about fifty yards above the woodpile on the false point, and held on the cabin under Plum Point till I raised the reef quarter—less twain—then straightened up for the middle bar till I got well abreast the old one-limbed cottonwood in the bend, then got my stern on the cottonwood and head on the low place above the point, and came through a-booming—nine and a half."

"Pretty square crossing, an't it?"

"Yes, but the upper bar's working down fast."

Another pilot spoke up and said:—

"I had better water than that and ran it lower down; started out from the false point—mark twain—raised the second reef abreast the big snag in the bend, and had quarter less twain."

One of the gorgeous ones remarked: "I don't want to find fault with your leadsmen, but that's a good deal of water for Plum Point, it seems to me."

There was an approving nod all around as this quiet snub dropped on the boaster and "settled" him. And so they went on talk-talk-talking. Meantime, the thing that was running in my mind was, "Now, if my ears hear aright, I have not only to get the names of all the towns and islands and bends, and so on, by heart, but I must even get up a warm personal acquaintanceship with every old snag and one-limbed cotton-wood and obscure wood-pile that ornaments the banks of this river for twelve hundred miles; and more than that, I must actually know where these things are in the dark, unless these guests are gifted with eyes that can pierce through two miles of solid blackness; I wish the piloting business was in Jericho and I had never thought of it."

At dusk Mr. Bixby tapped the big bell three times (the signal to land) and the captain emerged from his drawingroom in the forward end of the "texas," and looked up inquiringly. Mr. Bixby said:—

"We will lay up here all night, captain."

"Very well, sir."

That was all. The boat came to shore and was tied up for the night. It seemed to me a fine thing that the pilot could do as he pleased, without asking so grand a captain's permission. I took my supper and went immediately to bed, discouraged by my day's observations and experiences. My late voyage's notebooking was but a confusion of meaningless names. It had tangled me all up in a knot every time I had looked at it in the daytime. I now hoped for respite in sleep; but no, it reveled all through my head till sunrise again, a frantic and tireless nightmare.

Next morning I felt pretty rusty and low-spirited. We went booming along, taking a good many chances, for we were anxious to "get out of the river" (as getting out to Cairo was called) before night should overtake us. But Mr. Bixby's partner, the other pilot, presently grounded the boat, and we lost so much time getting her off that it was plain the darkness would overtake us a good long way above the mouth. This was a great misfortune, especially to certain of our visiting pilots, whose boats would have to wait for their return, no matter how long that might be. It sobered the pilot-house talk a good deal. Coming up-stream, pilots did not mind low water or any kind of darkness; nothing stopped them but fog. But down-stream work was different; a boat was too nearly helpless with a stiff current pushing behind her; so it was not customary to run down-stream at night in low water.

There seemed to be one small hope, however; if we could get through the intricate and dangerous Hat Island crossing before night, we could venture the rest, for we would have plainer sailing and better water. But it would be insanity to attempt Hat Island at night. So there was a deal of looking at watches all the rest of the day and a constant ciphering upon the speed we were making; Hat Island was the eternal subject; sometimes hope was high and sometimes we were delayed in a bad crossing, and down it went again. For hours all hands lay under the burden of this suppressed excitement; it was even communicated to me and I got to feeling so solicitous about Hat Island, and under such an awful pressure of responsibility, that I wished I might have five minutes on shore to draw a good, full, relieving breath and start over again. We were standing no regular watches. Each of our pilots ran such portions of the river as he had run when coming up-stream, because of his greater familiarity with it; but both remained in the pilot-house constantly.

An hour before sunset Mr. Bixby took the wheel and Mr. W—stepped aside. For the next thirty minutes every man held his watch in his hand and was restless, silent, and uneasy. At last somebody said, with a doomful sigh:

"Well, yonder's Hat Island—and we can't make it."

All the watches closed with a snap, everybody sighed and muttered something about its being "too bad, too bad—ah, if we could *only* have got here half an hour sooner!" and the place was thick with the atmosphere of disappointment. Some started to go out but loitered, hearing no bell-tap to land. The sun dipped behind the horizon, the boat went on. Inquiring looks passed from one guest to another; and one who had his hand on the doorknob and had turned it, waited, then presently took away his hand and let the knob turn back again. We bore steadily down the bend. More looks were exchanged and nods of surprised admiration— but no words. Insensibly the men drew together behind Mr. Bixby as the sky darkened and one or two dim stars came out. The dead silence and sense of waiting became oppressive. Mr. Bixby pulled the cord and two deep, mellow notes from the big bell floated off on the night. Then a pause, and one more note was struck. The watchman's voice followed, from the hurricane-deck:

"Labboard lead, there! Stabboard lead!"

The cries of the leadsmen began to rise out of the distance and were gruffly repeated by the word-passers on the hurricane-deck.

"M-a-r-k three! M-a-r-k three! Quarter-less-three! Half twain! Quarter twain! M-a-r-k twain! Quarter-less——"

Mr. Bixby pulled two bell-ropes and was answered by faint jinglings far below in the engine-room, and our speed slackened. The steam began to whistle through the gauge-cocks. The cries of the leadsmen went on—and it is a weird sound, always, in the night. Every pilot in the lot was watching now, with fixed eyes, and talking under his breath. Nobody was calm and easy but Mr. Bixby. He would put his wheel down and stand on a spoke, and as the steamer swung into her (to me) utterly invisible marks—for we seemed to be in the midst of a wide and gloomy sea—he would meet and fasten her there. Talk was going on, now, in low voices:—

"There; she's over the first reef all right!"

After a pause, another subdued voice:—

"Her stern's coming down just *exactly* right, by *George*! Now she's in the marks; over she goes!"

Somebody else muttered:

"Oh, it was done beautiful—*beautiful*!"

Now the engines were stopped altogether and we drifted with the current. Not that I could see the boat drift, for I could not, the stars being all gone by this time. This drifting was the dismalest work; it held one's heart still. Presently I discovered a blacker gloom than that which surrounded us. It was the head of the island. We were closing right down upon it. We entered its deeper shadow, and so imminent seemed the peril that I was likely to suffocate; and I had the strongest impulse to do *something*, anything, to save the vessel. But still Mr. Bixby stood by his wheel, silent, intent as a cat, and all the pilots stood shoulder to shoulder at his back.

"She'll not make it!" somebody whispered.

The water grew shoaler and shoaler by the leadsman's cries, till it was down to—

"Eight-and-a-half! E-i-g-h-t feet! E-i-g-h-t feet! Seven-and——"

Mr. Bixby said warningly through his speaking-tube to the engineer:

"Stand by, now!"

"Ay, ay, sir!"

"Seven-and-a-half! Seven feet! *Six*-and——"

We touched bottom! Instantly Mr. Bixby set a lot of bells ringing, shouted through the tube, "*Now*, let her have it—every ounce you've got!" then to his partner, "Put her hard down! snatch her! snatch her!" The boat rasped and ground her way through the sand, hung upon the apex of disaster a singly tremendous instant, and then over she went! And such a shout as went up at Mr. Bixby's back never loosened the roof of a pilot-house before!

There was no more trouble after that. Mr. Bixby was a hero that night; and it was some little time, too, before his exploit ceased to be talked about by river-men.

Fully to realize the marvelous precision required in laying the great steamer in her marks in that murky waste of water, one should know that not only must she pick her intricate way through snags and blind reefs, and then shave the head of the island so closely as to brush the overhanging foliage with her stern, but at one place she must pass almost within arm's reach of a sunken and invisible wreck that would snatch the hull timbers from under her if she should strike it, and destroy a quarter of a million dollars' worth of steamboat and cargo in five minutes, and maybe a hundred and fifty human lives into the bargain.

The last remark I heard that night was a compliment to Mr. Bixby, uttered in soliloquy and with unction by one of our guests. He said:—

"By the Shadow of Death, but he's a lightning pilot!"

COMPOSITION ASSIGNMENT

Plan a reminiscent, or retrospective, essay. The various essays in this section should suggest possibilities of subject matter and treatment. Most students

The second major episode of the chapter is not merely a second example of what has been previously demonstrated, for in at least two ways there is a progression beyond what was communicated at the end of section 28. First, from the point of view of the author and the reader, the two demonstrations of skill differ in degree; secondly, the cub's reactions to the two episodes are seen to differ.

The reader will appreciate the first point if he has observed the difference between the attitude of all but the cub as the landing at Jones's plantation is discussed and later accomplished (pages 85, 87–88) and the attitude of the other pilots toward the Hat Island crossing.

(c) *Explain the difference.*

The reader will appreciate the second point if he has observed the difference in the cub's reactions to the two accomplishments.

(d) *How has his regard for his mentor and his occupation changed?*

Now refer to the third from last paragraph.

(e) *The paragraph is an example of which of the kinds of writing discussed in Section 1?*
(f) *From what point of view is the paragraph written?*
(g) *What does the paragraph contribute to the development of Twain's chapter, "Learning the River"?*
(h) *Is there any reason that it is better placed where it is than at the very end?*

When the reader perceives the lines of development discussed above, he sees that Twain's chapter is not a loose collection of episodes, but a coherent whole. In addition to giving the reader impressions of a bygone way of life, it presents a unified and will recall an introduction to, and possible mastery of, a sport or other activity, for example, camping, sailing, skiing; or debating, learning a musical instrument, struggling with algebra, or coping with a summer job. Many will associate these experiences with an interesting person or place.

Try to remain aware of your point of view; as you recall your experiences, are you looking at them as you saw them at the time or as you now understand them? If you choose an experience far enough back in time so that you are aware of differences between past and present attitudes, you can create the kind of interest that Mark Twain has created through the interplay of the two points of view.

This is intended to be a major assignment culminating your study of narrative-descriptive writing. It may be approached in various ways. You may be asked to submit a sentence outline before you write the essay (see page 25), or you may be asked to choose a broad topic and write several short pieces on different aspects of it, for example, a description of setting, a character sketch, then a narrative of an episode. You may then be asked to combine these materials into a coherent whole.

climactic account of a stage in the development of young Sam Clemens.

(i) *The title "Learning the River" gives only a superficial idea of what the chapter is about. Write a title which gives a better idea of its theme.*

EXPOSITORY WRITING—INFORMATION

4 | *Expository Writing—Information*

The selections of Section 3 have in common the purpose of sharing impressions and recollections with the reader. He retains impressions not only of the subject matter but also of the personality of the writer, that is, of his characteristic interests, attitudes, and temperament.

The selections of Section 4 differ from the preceding ones in that the purpose of their authors is to inform the reader about matters in which the authors have some degree of expertness. They combine description and exposition to explain what lies beyond the experience or knowledge of most readers and probably would not be clear to most readers on casual observation of the subject.

THE WAYS OF A BEAR

Paul B. Kinney

[1] Folklore and imaginative fiction have so distorted our conception of the bear that the real animal is hardly recognizable when met and observed in the forest. Equipped by Nature with a huge body, powerful muscles, large claw-studded paws, and long glistening teeth, the American black bear might be expected to be a predator, a carnivorous mammal, horrible to behold, a menace to all life, an animal from whom even man should flee in terror.

[2] In reality, he is neither vicious nor pugnacious. He is omnivorous and will eat anything, although he shows a predilection for vegetable matter. Not alone in his food, but in his behavior also, the black bear is a paradox. He is both the most interesting and the most baffling of wild animals.

[3] Highly intelligent, inconsistent, and often impulsive, he is wholly unpredictable in his actions. He is the clown of the forest. He will climb a tree simply to slide down a branch like a boy sliding down the banister. He will fight a ferocious battle with a small bush and then strut off as if he had conquered the world. He has a world of self-respect and dignity in the presence of others, yet alone he becomes a rollicking, hilarious prankster with a sense of humor and imagination that is decidedly mischievous.

[1] (a) *Would you classify this paragraph as description, exposition, or a combination of both?*
(b) *How is the paragraph developed?*
(c) *In the first sentence, what does "our" indicate of the author's assumptions about his audience?*

[2] (a) *Explain the transition between paragraphs. Apart from the opening phrase, what words relate the paragraph to the preceding one?*
(b) *Might the first two paragraphs be combined? Is there any advantage in the separation?*

[3] *Explain the relationship between this and the preceding paragraphs.*

[1]–[3] The first three paragraphs constitute an introduction.

(a) *Which sentence in one of them serves as a topic sentence for all three paragraphs?*
(b) *What is the chief purpose and effect of the introduction?*

[4] Born during hibernation, in late January or early February, the black bear weighs then about half a pound. Ten years later, when he reaches his prime, he may weigh four hundred pounds, or more. Except for the marsupials, the bear at birth is the smallest of mammals in proportion to the adult size, yet he becomes the largest of our fur-bearing animals.

[4] **(a)** *What principle might have led a writer to begin the essay at this point? What would be the disadvantage in doing so?*
(b) *How does the paragraph continue the theme of the introduction?*

[5] During his first year, a bear cub's life is idyllic. Fed and protected by an adoring, self-forgetful mother, the cub eats, sleeps, and grows fat. Of cares, he has none.

[6] Contrary to popular conception, a mother bear does not abuse her cub. She is a strict disciplinarian and does not hesitate to punish disobedience. Experience has taught her that a headstrong cub soon comes to grief if its enthusiasm is not curbed. But she is neither cruel nor vicious with her chastisements. I have seen an adventuresome and disobedient cub knocked down by a large male, and have seen the mother, with utter disregard for herself, dash to the protection of her offspring, only to be in turn mauled by the male bear. Then, when her mission had been accomplished and the cub saved, I have seen her kiss him and search tenderly for injuries before ever attending to her own stinging wounds.

[6] *How does the first sentence contribute to the unity, coherence, and emphasis of the essay?*

[7] However, mother love—intense, self-sacrificial, tender almost to a fault—is short-lived. By the second spring it burns itself out and grows cold. Mating season in California is June. Before that time arrives mother bear, her instincts having turned to the coming generation, drives her cubs into the forest, and from that day will never again recognize them as her own flesh and blood.

[7] *How does this paragraph combine with 6 to develop the topic sentence of paragraphs 1–3?*

8 As a yearling, the black bear begins his solitary life in the forest. The whole forest is now his home. He does not have a den to which he returns periodically to sleep. He sleeps where and when he feels sleepy, usually during the heat of the day, often upon some high boulder, a fallen log, or among the branches of a tree. He eats what he finds, where he finds it. Regardless of whether he is the only bear on his particular range, or whether he lives in a thickly populated area, as in one of our National Parks, the black bear is an individualist and remains such throughout his life.

4–**8** (a) *What kind of order governs the presentation of details in these paragraphs?* (b) *Which of the kinds of writing do we have here?*

9 While the behavior of individuals may differ slightly, and the habits vary with the region, general traits of the black bear are similar wherever found. When necessity demands, a bear, with rare exceptions, proves himself courageous. He is a bluffer without equal; an artist who will go to no end of trouble to accomplish a successful bluff. Of course, a bluff that leads to a battle is not a success.

9 The mention of a specific trait introduces a sequence of paragraphs which illustrate the trait through an anecdote (see pages 104–106). Such illustrations are often useful in exposition.

10 It is a great privilege to watch two accomplished bluffers meet on a bear trail in the forest. With a hundred yards separating them, the first bear will sit down and stare off through the trees. The other, not to be outdone, suddenly finds an unusually interesting patch of sunlight that he proceeds to investigate.

10–**17** (a) *According to what kind of relationship are the details of this sequence of paragraphs arranged?* (b) *By itself, this sequence is an example of which kind of writing?*

11 Five minutes pass. The first bear heaves a big sigh, rises slowly and with a great show of indifference, moves off the trail, examines a stump and returns aimlessly to the trail again. By this time the other has decided the sun patch cannot be eaten, and he too returns to the trail.

12 Neither has yet given the slightest indication, by act or expression, that he is aware of the other's presence. Each, however, is secretly watching the other's movements, and the hundred yards that separated them has dwindled to fifty. This strange pantomine of pretended unawareness is repeated, and possibly half an hour after they first sighted each other, twenty yards still separates the two.

[13] Suddenly, unable to stand the suspense longer, one breaks the silence of the forest with a loud snort. The other, pretending great surprise, stops dead in the trail. He may chop his jaws in an ominous manner, or may simply sit down, apparently thinking over the situation.

[14] Another five minutes pass with no offensive gestures other than the hollow clicking of teeth as each bear wags his head and chops his jaws. Both appear bored to death, yet each enjoys the game hugely.

[15] Presently, the suspense becomes too great for one, and he waddles stiff-legged toward his opponent. This is the first sign of weakening. Fear plays no part, for both are courageous, but suspense often breaks nerves that would remain calm in actual combat. Before he has lessened the distance by half, the bear veers off the trail and slaps viciously at a bush. The other may sit or stand quietly, pretending to watch a deer in the meadow.

[16] Suddenly, the first bear makes a lunge, his paws making a mighty thud as he slaps the ground and stops short of his opponent. Then, with mouths agape, heads held low and turned slightly, both bears bellow like cows. The forest resounds to their roars, and one expects a titanic battle to ensue.

[16] *How does the last sentence remind us of the main theme of the essay?*

[17]   Presently the less proficient bluffer steps cautiously aside, and continuing his threatening jaw chopping, makes off, his dignity preserved and his hide intact.   The other, shaking his head, sad that the game is over, waddles aimlessly along the trail he was following when interrupted.

[18]   The American black bear is not so industrious as his cousin, the grizzly bear, but although he appears to be an idler, he is not. His sense of smell and hearing are unusually keen.   Far from being the dumb brute that many suppose, he is a resourceful thinker.   He is anxious to learn, and he immediately investigates in a thorough and intelligent manner each unusual situation that arouses his curiosity.

[18]   *How does this paragraph pick up both the introductory formula and the main theme?*

[19]   When the bear eats, the bars are down, and woe to the unwary camper who leaves food unguarded.   He has catholic tastes, a magnificent appetite, an enormous capacity, and a digestive tract that must be leather-lined.   He eats anything he can get and all he can get of it.   Bruin has few inhibitions where food is concerned. It may be bitter, sweet or tart; green or ripe; dry or juicy.   He asks only that it be edible— not digestible, simply edible.   Skunk cabbage, the juice of which might just as well be sulphuric acid; bitter cherries, that taste like a mixture of alum and quinine—these he will eat with gusto, smack his lips and look for more.

[20]   All in all, the life habits of the American black bear constitute one of the most interesting, amusing, and, at times, baffling studies of wild life.   But it is such things that add zest, and flavor pleasantly the study of Nature.   In the process of taking one wild life photograph, a person learns far more about the animal than if he had collected a dozen specimens with a gun.

[20] (a)   *Has the content of the essay justified the author's use in his conclusion of each of the adjectives modifying "studies"?*
(b)   *Is the last sentence an effective part of the summation of the essay, or is it an* **irrelevance**—*a violation of unity, coherence, and emphasis?*

COMPOSITION ASSIGNMENT

Write an essay which, like "The Ways of the Bear," is intended to interest the general reader and inform him about some subject with which you are thoroughly familiar. Animals, whether tame or wild, are an obvious possibility. However, do not write a character sketch of an individual such as "My Mutt Rover," but rather an essay on the traits of a breed such as "Poodles Are Intelligent Creatures." Other possibilities are natural phenomena and the activities of various groups of people. Remember that your principal purpose is to convey information.

Two Examples of
The Presentation of Scientific Information

The premise of informative writing is that the author's purpose is to communicate special knowledge to a reader who does not possess it. To do so effectively, he must determine how much basic knowledge he can expect of the audience he wishes to reach, and he must choose his language accordingly. A physicist who wishes to present the results of his research to a group of physicists can use the language of physics. If he wishes to present his findings to an audience of non-specialists who have a basic scientific education and an active interest in science, he cannot depend upon a knowledge of terminology peculiar to physics, but may use a basic scientific vocabulary that he could not use if writing for a more general public. The following two excerpts from "What You Should Know About Physics" and from "Your Brain and Your Behavior," while more technical and more demanding than "The Ways of a Bear," are less technical than works written for specialists. They show some of the ways in which the specialist may make his topic comprehensible to an audience of non-specialists.

From WHAT YOU SHOULD
KNOW ABOUT PHYSICS

Sir George Thomson

[1] Let us now consider the three theories of light, which introduce the paradox that scientific principles can be something other than either true or false. They can be true, in other words, to a degree.

[1] *What sort of audience do the title and the first paragraph seem to assume?*

[2] The ray theory of light says that light goes in straight lines called rays. These rays, however, can be reflected by a mirror or refracted at a transparent surface such as water. The Greeks knew about the laws of reflection; the laws of refraction were established early in the seventeenth century.

[2] *Are "reflection" and "refraction" equally comprehensible terms, or is one less likely than the other to be understood by a reader unfamiliar with basic physics?*

③ The wave theory of light, conceived by Huygens of The Hague late in the seventeenth century, says that light is a wave motion in some sort of ether. This ether, at first thought to be an elastic substance which permeated all matter, later came to be considered as something which acted electromagnetically. The wave theory was placed on a firm mathematical basis early in the nineteenth century and until recently was accepted by physicists as the principle which best explained the properties of light.

④ During the early years of this century the extraordinary behavior of x-rays and of various types of radiation from hot, solid bodies forced on physicists a new set of ideas called the quantum theory. The quantum theory supposes that the action of one body on another occurs, not smoothly and uniformly, but by discontinuous steps. Light is emitted and absorbed in discrete packets—the energy of each packet being determined by the wave length, or color, of the light. In considering the properties of light the quantum theory combines this new concept with elements of the ray and the wave concepts and certain revolutionary assumptions of quantum mechanics which introduce the element of indeterminacy into man's conception of the universe.

③ (a) *Do you think any of the terms used in the paragraph would be likely to create difficulty for the reader referred to above?* (b) *Can you think of any sort of comparison that would help the general reader to see what is meant by "wave motion in some sort of ether"?*

④ (a) *The paragraph contains an explanation of "quantum theory." Does the explanation contain any word that is not clear to you from context?* (b) *Do you understand how man's concept of the universe has been affected by the "element of indeterminacy"?*

It is only fair to say that, after concluding this section about the three theories of light, the author presents a section on indeterminacy. However, the above questions still have a bearing on the matter of the effectiveness of the paragraph and the section of the essay from which they come.

From YOUR BRAIN AND YOUR BEHAVIOR

R. W. Gerard

[1] Modern science, winning its way into the mysteries of nature, is now facing one of its sternest challenges. Does man's psyche—mind and sentience, will and purpose—lie beyond the scope of science? Or are the inimitable properties of man, whence flow the magnificent achievements of humanity, the outcome of comprehensible processes, which can be explained through the disciplines of science? In search of an answer, we must turn to the relationship between brain and behavior.

[1] The first paragraph introduces a question which reveals that the author, as is characteristic of essayists, is concerned, not merely with the facts, but with the implications of those facts. Such an introduction can create and focus interest. Note that it differs from the sort of introduction which merely presents a brief preliminary statement of what is to be developed in the body of the essay.

What term is defined, and by what method?

[2] A guided missile behaves as if it has purpose. It "seeks its goal" or evades a hazard, even though the maneuvers required twist its path like a pretzel. Such goal-seeking, self-regulating devices are known to engineers as servomechanisms. Neurophysiologists today are wondering whether the nervous system is no more than this.

[2] **(a)** *How does the author introduce the definition of "servomechanism"?*
(b) *Is the informal phrase "twist its path like a pretzel" a strength or a weakness?*
(c) *Must the reader bring to the essay a knowledge of what a neurophysiologist is, or is his speciality sufficiently clear from the context?*

[3] Whether more or not, the human brain is at least a marvelously spun servomechanism that can outperform its own inventions. The airman on a team of physicists and engineers is right when he objects to the idea that airplanes are now so automatically controlled that the pilot can practically be eliminated. "Before you throw out the pilot," he asks, "consider where else can you get a highly modifiable, versatile servomechanism, weighing only one hundred and fifty pounds, produced so cheaply by completely unskilled labor?"

[3] *What purpose other than offering a bit of humor is served by the introduction of the airman's question?*

4 A submarine, too, acts like a single living thing. It seems to show unified purpose. It keeps to a course, it corrects its errors. Yet the submarine and its machinery and cargo are products of many men, just as its crew is composed of many individuals. The structures and the functions of the many coordinate to form a larger unity, with a character and personality of its own. Any component may change—engines may be replaced, superstructure remodeled, hull repaired, crew rotated, a new captain placed in command—without interrupting the life course of the whole.

5 A submarine is like a man, at a different level. For a man, too, is composed of many individuals and their products, forming a greater whole with its own individuality. When egg and sperm unite, the single resulting cell divides into two cells, each of which in turn divide into two, and so on for some forty cell generations. The total number of cells so formed in a single human is a thousand times greater than the world's population. Under proper conditions each cell can survive separately. Some manufacture non-living products—horn, hair, bone, blood, tendon. As cells develop they specialize in forming different tissues and organs. Muscle cells differ vastly from skin cells. Liver cells and kidney cells, both concerned with chemical changes, are readily distinguishable under the microscope.

6 The cells in the nervous system especially concerned with behavior are called neurones. Most cells resemble packed spheres, like marshmallows pressed together in a bag. They may lie close together, or they may be separated by fluids or by strands of fibrous material. Whether close or separate, they have little more immediate relationship then strangers in a crowd. Neurones are different. Extensions from their

4 This paragraph provides the basis of the **analogy** completed in the next paragraph. An analogy is a kind of comparison often used to clarify the nature of an object or concept under discussion. Most analogies are built upon similarities of function (the way things work) and most embody more than one point of resemblance. Usually the analogy is made from something abstract and complex to something more tangible, more readily perceived.

5 *In your opinion, does this paragraph contain terms or concepts beyond the range of the high school student?*

6 This paragraph introduces and defines three terms which designate special kinds of nerve cells.

(a) *Explain how the technique of **differentiation** is employed in the definition of the first term.*
(b) *Is the marshmallow comparison an analogy? Why, or why not?*
(c) *Is the spider comparison an analogy? Why, or why not?*

roughly spherical cell bodies make contact with other neurones, often far distant, and carry messages to or from them. Think of a spider suspended from a roof by a long slender strand, its several legs extending from its body. Reduced manyfold it somewhat resembles a neurone. The long strand suggests the axone, as in man's sciatic nerve, a single, thin, protoplasmic thread that constitutes an unbroken expressway for zooming nerve messages; the leg suggest the dendrites, shorter receiving branches that convey messages to the cell body.

Note that the last comparison leads naturally into the definition of the second term.

(d) *What means are used to define the second term?*

(e) *Would you expect to find the expressway metaphor in a dictionary or textbook definition of "axone"?*

(f) *By what method is the third term defined?*

(g) *Finally, list the means of definition used in this paragraph and in paragraphs 1 and 2.*

[7] These neurone strands comprise set paths linked to other neurones within the nervous system and form the nerves connecting to outside structures. Nerves from the sense organs bring information to the brain; nerves to effectors, such as muscles and glands, carry instructions for action. Normally, our muscles contract only when aroused by nerve messages, and these must be sent from the appropriate neurones. In taking a simple step, for example, several dozen muscles must contract and relax at the proper moments and in the proper strengths, and the neurones that control them must send their signals in precise patterns of time and space. When many potential connections become effective simultaneously, as occurs under strychnine poisoning, any incoming nerve message—even one from a gentle stroking of the skin—can discharge into so many channels that practically all the muscles are activated at once, and convulsion results.

(The essay continues through further explanation of the functions of the nervous system to a discussion of the implications suggested in the opening paragraph.)

[7] This paragraph proceeds from analysis of the parts to an explanation of the operation of the system as a whole.

What is the method by which the meaning of "effector" is made clear even though the term is not actually defined?

SUMMARY

The two preceding selections are taken from a collection of magazine articles published by the *Saturday Evening Post* to help bridge the "gap between the intellectual and the intelligent layman." (Such articles are often called "popularizations.")

Is one of the two selections more successful in arousing the interest or meeting the needs of the intended audience? If you feel that one is superior, be prepared to explain why.

Which of the two do you think is of greater value as a demonstration of techniques useful in writing intended to communicate your special knowledge to an audience unfamiliar with your speciality?

COMPOSITION ASSIGNMENT

Choose a subject about which you have more knowledge than the general reader and write a technical exposition of some aspect of it. Your knowledge should come from personal experience rather than from the classroom, a textbook, or a reference work. Make use of some of the terms of your specialty and define or explain them in such a way as to preserve the coherence of the exposition. Keep in mind the possibilities of the techniques used in the preceding excerpts. Sciences, sports, hobbies— all should provide suitable subjects.

From ROADS TO FREEDOM

Bertrand Russell

The previous selections are essays dealing with tangible, or concrete, subjects. They serve as a useful reminder that the writer must keep his reader in mind and must clarify the terms he uses; in other words, he must define. Especially when we are discussing abstract concepts, about which there is likely to be a divergence of opinion, we may need to define a term at length, as Bertrand Russell does with "socialism" in the following paragraph. The term so defined is apt to be an abstract one, about which there is divergence of opinion. The paragraph of definition will usually set up the limits within which the meaning of the term falls. It will do so by giving a general heading under which the term can be listed and then by making a series of distinctions between the term defined and other words under the same heading.

Socialism, like everything else that is vital, is rather a tendency than a strictly definable body of doctrine. A definition of Socialism is sure either to include some views which many would regard as not Socialistic, or to exclude others which claim to be included. But I think we shall come nearest to the essence of Socialism by defining it as the advocacy of communal ownership of land and capital. Communal ownership may mean ownership by a democratic State, but cannot be held to include ownership by any State which is not democratic. Communal ownership may also be understood,

(a) *What is the key word in the opening statement about socialism?*
(b) *What comment does the second sentence make on the problem of definition?*

Sentence 3 gives the general heading under which distinctions are to be made.

(c) *What is the general heading?*
(d) *The next two sentences establish what relationship between socialism and government?*

The next two sentences extend the boundaries of the term.

as Anarchist Communism understands it, in the sense of ownership by the free association of the men and women in a community without those compulsory powers which are necessary to constitute a State. Some Socialists expect communal ownership to arrive suddenly and completely by catastrophic revolution, while others expect it to come gradually, first in one industry, then in another. Some insist upon the necessity of completeness in the acquisition of land and capital by the public, while others would be content to see lingering islands of private ownership, provided they were not too expensive or powerful. What all forms have in common is democracy and the abolition, virtual or complete, of the present capitalistic system. The distinction between Socialists, Anarchists and Syndicalists turns largely upon the kind of democracy which they desire. Orthodox Socialists are content with parliamentary democracy in the sphere of government, holding that the evils apparent in this form of constitution at present would disappear with the disappearance of capitalism. Anarchists and Syndicalists, on the other hand, object to the whole parliamentary machinery, and aim at a different method of regulating the political affairs of the community. But all alike are democratic in the sense that they aim at abolishing every kind of privilege and every kind of artificial inequality: all alike are champions of the wage earner in existing society. All three also have much in common in their economic doctrine. All three regard capital and the wage system as a means of exploiting the laborer in the interests of the possessing classes, and hold that communal ownership, in one form or another, is the only means of bringing freedom to the producers. But within the framework of this common doctrine there are many divergences, and even among those who are strictly to be called Socialists, there is a very considerable diversity of schools.

(e) *The sentence which begins "What all forms have in common. . . ." serves what purpose?*

The next three sentences follow the same pattern as the three previous sentences.

(f) *What definition is implied for "democratic"?*

The remainder of the paragraph deals with "economic doctrine."

(g) *What is the purpose of the last sentence?*

COMPOSITION ASSIGNMENT

Write a one-paragraph definition of an abstract term about which there is enough variety of opinion to warrant a definition. Possible subjects are school spirit, sportsmanship, physical or moral courage, student government.

THE BEE'S KNEES

Charles D. Stewart

The preceding excerpts introduce the reader to appropriate technical terms as they present specialized information. The following essay takes a different approach. It presents highly technical information about the anatomy and behavior of bees, but it does so without employing the technical language that specialists use.

The structure of the essay is also interesting to students of composition. It differs from "The Ways of a Bear" in following an organization based on the principle of **partition,** the systematic division of the broad topic into its subordinate parts. It therefore provides an opportunity to study and apply a method of organization appropriate to much expository writing.

I

[1] A bee in the field is engaged in gathering three sorts of raw material: flour, varnish, and syrup—all of them commodities which present problems in handling and transportation.

[2] That the yellow pollen of the flowers is simply flour to a bee may be gathered from the fact that beekeepers, in seasons when pollen is scarce, set out little troughs of rye flour which serves the bees instead and induces them to

The Topical Outline

One kind of outlining, the "sentence outline," has been explained in Section 2 (second paragraph of Summary, page 25). Another kind, probably already familiar to you, is the **topical outline,** which employs numerals and letters followed by words or phrases to indicate the subdivision of the essay into main topics and subtopics. Such an outline is an

raise young earlier in the season than they otherwise would. Young bees, like young children, cannot thrive and develop on sweets alone; and so the pollen, a highly nitrogenous product, is the food of the young bee during the days when it is truly a baby in the cradle, occupying the open cell in larval form. Honey, a form of sugar, supplies the bee, as it does the human worker, with a vast amount of heat and energy; but it lacks the elements needed in repair and growth. The older bees eat the pollen in small quantity also, a certain proportion of it being necessary to health.

[3] As for varnish, the bee gets hers from the same source that man does—the resinous exudation of trees. But the bee finds the readiest supply on sticky buds such as those of the balm of Gilead tree, and, in lesser quantity, on the buds of poplar, horse chestnut, willow, and hollyhock. While we are accustomed to think of the bee as a hoarder of honey, entirely possessed with her passion for sweets, the fact is that every worker bee has varnish on her mind. She will gather it as eagerly and hurry home with it in as high a state of happiness as if she were working in nectar or in pollen. A swarm of bees that has found suitable quarters in the decayed hollow of a tree will clean it out scrupulously, removing every particle of loose dirt and rubbish, and may then repair its surface until they have given it a complete coat of varnish. Those that are kept in the usual "patent" hives stop up every crack and crevice with their resin; and they cement the lid on so tight that the beekeeper has to carry a special tool to pry it off. Mixed with wax it makes the wax stickier and hardens it, and this preparation they use as a basis and buttress with which to fasten their combs securely. If a mouse, or other large unwieldy animal, invades the hive and dies there, a problem in sanitary engineering

excellent device for taking notes on the expository writing for which students are responsible in various school courses; it ensures a grasp of the relationship between idea and clarifying or supporting detail. It is also a valuable means of organizing one's own writing, especially when, as in much informative writing, the material can be classified—that is, logically subdivided.

To help you master the technique, the first section of "The Bee's Knees" has been outlined, and you will be asked to make a similar outline of the second.

The topical outline is an accurate analysis or a useful plan only if the topics are listed so as to show the place of a topic in a scheme of organization extending from the most general to the most specific. In the outline that follows, capital letters are used to designate the major subdivisions of the author's section I. Thus entries A and B are **subordinate** to I and **coordinate** with each other. Under A, the arabic numerals 1, 2, and 3 designate subtopics of A that are coordinate with each other. Subdivisions of these topics are designated by lower-case letters. When still further subdivision is required, lower-case roman numerals are used. The basis of topical outlining, then, is the use of one kind of numeral or letter to designate topics which are coordinate with each other and subordinate to a broader topic.

The following is the first part of an outline of section I of "The Bee's Knees." Observe that the paragraph divisions do not, and need not, correspond with the numbering of the topics. The author has given a single paragraph to topics 1 and 3, but the relative complexity of topic 2 and the desire to introduce the anecdote have led him to present the topic in three paragraphs.

has to be met and dealt with. Varnish-gatherers set to work at once, and in a short time they have the mouse coated over and made odorless—virtually embalmed in their sweet-smelling resins. Usually bees deal with any objectionable object by dragging it out of the door and casting it overboard; but there are cases when such measures are not practicable.

[4] Some years ago, on a bright warm day in spring, I set to work to varnish a sponson canoe and get it in shape for another season's use on the lake on which I live. I had not plied the brush long when I became aware that a number of bees were keeping me company. Then more and more bees. After a while they became so numerous, and were flying about in such a highly excited state of mind, that I put down the brush and began to worry. At that time I knew a great deal about bees, or thought I did; and so I was perfectly aware that bees gather the resinous propolis at great expenditure of time and labor. But up to the time when I met the bees in a common concern over the same sort of work, I did not really know what I had learned. This "propolis" was a word which kept itself in a different department of my mind from that in which I deal with my everyday work; and so I did not know, as these particular bees did, that it was the same sort of stuff that I was putting on my canoe. But then—who would ever suspect that a bee could know so much about Greek! This little episode taught me a lesson in writing; I decided that if I ever wrote anything about bees I would use the plain word "varnish."

[5] A bee carries her varnish in her pollen basket, so called because she also packs her flour in it. She gathers it when it is in such a warm, sticky condition that it will draw out in a thread; and when she has loaded up with all the sticky stuff she can handle, she hurries home

I. The Work of the Bee

   A. Gathering of Raw Materials

[1]   Introductory list

[2]   1. Pollen (flour)
       a. Nature
       b. Use
     2. Propolis (varnish)

[3]   a. Sources and uses
         i. Sources
         ii. Uses

[4]   b. Explanatory anecdote
         i. Nature of propolis
         ii. Basis of author's style*

[5]   c. Bee's handling of propolis

[6]   3. Nectar (syrup)
       a. Source
       b. Uses
         i. Own food
         ii. Food for workers in hive
         iii. Food for later use

---

* As you read on, observe how the principle expressed in 2, b, ii governs the author's choice of words to describe the bee's specialized parts and functions.

and applies it to the hive while it is yet in a workable state. Commercial beekeepers, when they have worked a while with their hives, taking off lids and handling frames, find their hands covered with a gummy tenacious substance which soap and water has little effect upon. Following the advice of their Langstroth, or other work on practical beekeeping, they use turpentine or alcohol to get it off. A bee's varnish resembles man's in the embarrassing qualities of stickiness and insolubility, and so, if a bee can get it off her bristly body without using any special recipe out of a bee book, I think it is evident that she knows how to handle varnish. I am quite willing to believe that she could make use of canoe varnish, even though it is guaranteed to set dust free in a few hours and to be glass hard in a day or two.

6 The nectar from the blossoms is the bee's true food. While much of it finds its way into her stomach to supply her present needs, much more is retained in her honey bag, or crop, to be carried home in the form of sap and evaporated to honey in the cells. A bee that is engaged in field work never eats honey so long as the nectar is to be had. She simply stores it up for future use, and for the support of the bees that work in the hive. As a certain part of the swarm, the younger bees, stay at home and devote themselves to household specialties— wax-making, comb-building, nursing, and ventilating—they have to be supported on honey by the workers in the field. This current consumption alone is enough to keep them busy, especially when there is comb being built; besides which there must be a good supply of honey sealed up for time of need.

7 In hot weather a number of bees in every hive are acting in the capacity of electric fans, their wings working away at a great rate while

7 This paragraph begins the second major subdivision (B) of section I.

(a) *Is the transition adequate?*
(b) *Write a transitional sentence that will be a more explicit guide to the structure of this section.*
(c) *Do you think an improvement would result from inclusion of your sentence?*

they drive the air in just the directions needed in a well-calculated ventilating system. In front of any hive, holding their proper stations at the narrow entrance, a detachment of these ventilating bees may be seen. Their heads are always turned toward the entrance so that the air is kept moving past them toward the rear, the reason for this position being that these bees are drawing out the foul air from the hive. On the inside of the hive, their heads turned also toward the entrance, is another file of bees propelling the air past them toward the interior. These bees are sucking in fresh air to take the place of the foul air. It is a double ventilating system based upon good mechanical principles.

8 To get the full effect of ventilation, it is not enough to admit a steady supply of fresh air at such an opening; it is also desirable to keep the whole mass of air in motion. Building engineers who specialize on such problems as are presented by theatres, moving picture houses, and other human hives, have recently announced as an interesting discovery that there is a vivifying influence imparted to air simply by keeping it in motion, and this in addition to, or independent of, any new supply of oxygen. Whether there is any truth in these conclusions or not, bees fulfill all the requirements necessary to take advantage of them, for inside the hive are other detachments of bees steadily agitating the air. A bee has two pairs of wings, the rear pair and the forward pair being placed so close together that their edges almost touch. The wings are hooked together in flying, and to this end there is a row of little hooks on the forward edge of the rear wing and a stiff pleat on the edge of the front wing in which the little hooks may readily engage. A single pair of broad wings would be quite as serviceable in flying, but such a pair would not

The following continues the outline of section I.

    B. Ventilation of the Hive
        1. Mechanics
           a. Functions
             i. Intake and exhaust

8

             ii. Agitation of internal air
           b. Adaptation of the bee for ventilation

At this point, study the relationship between the logical structure, as represented by the outline, and the paragraph structure. The main idea of the paragraph is the importance of keeping in motion the air inside the hive. The second part of the paragraph, on the bee's wings, is presented as subordinate to this main idea. Would it be more logical to present this second part as a separate paragraph?

go into a cell. For this purpose they unhook and fold together like a fan. It has been observed that, in ventilating, bees do not have the wings hooked together.

[9] The effect of this well-directed activity is not only to give a supply of life-sustaining oxygen to the multitude of workers in the hive, but also to keep down the temperature when there is danger of the comb melting, and in addition, to evaporate the surplus water from the honey stored in the cells, which are never sealed shut till the product is properly "ripened." The nectar in some seasons is more watery than at other periods; but whatever its condition in this regard, the bees bring it in and store it in the open cells and then fan it to the right consistency. The watery product is held in the uncapped cells largely by capillary attraction; but the bees have a tendency to build the cells with a dip toward the rear. When they are building cells especially for the storage of honey this dip is more pronounced, as if they considered it an advantage; but they also use brood cells which have hatched their young and been cleaned out, and here the tendency is not so pronounced. The practice of building the caps from the bottom up, after the manner of a dam, also helps them in filling the cells full without leakage. Their care in evaporating the honey till it is a highly concentrated food-product is an economic one, due to the high cost of wax. It takes from seven to fifteen pounds of honey to make one pound of wax, and this means that, in addition to all the time and energy spent in gathering the honey, there is the time spent in digesting it into wax. They cannot afford to use such an expensive product for the storage of water.

[10] As this work of driving air in and out of the door is very exhausting, other bees take the

[9] The following continues the outline of section I, B.

   2. Purposes
     a. Oxygen supply
     b. Temperature control
     c. Evaporation of surplus water

[10]
   3. A mysterious cooperative effort

places of any that have grown tired, and so the ventilating crew gradually changes. The hotter the day or the more liquid the nectar, the more fanning there is in the hive. If the entrance is stopped up, by way of experiment, the whole populace will set their wings a-going. It is apparent that the ventilating bees are not specialists, except as they specialize for a while on this part of the work. They are volunteers, taking their places among the files at the entrance or manning the forces of the interior as circumstances require. And what influence is it, or what supreme authority, that picks this bee and that one for the task, sets some to fanning the interior, sends others to complete the files of the fresh air crew or the foul air gang, and keeps up the balanced quota at the door? I am afraid we shall have to call this a mystery.

[11] Indeed, we have now been led to the point where all study of bees, in any of their various activities, must inevitably lead us. At first we are shrewd observers, duly careful and skeptical in our conclusions, but led on by fact after fact until, just as we are about to reach the point of knowledge, we must admit that we are baffled. Unless we throw our scientific caution to the winds and turn poet or romancer, there is little to do but wonder. And I do not know but this latter outcome marks a man's deepest knowledge of nature. Especially as the wonder must beget a certain reverence, and a due humility of mind in the presence of the unknowable.

II

[12] A bee needs so many tools in the day's work—such a variety of combs, brushes, pincers, shears, and what not—that her body is fairly covered with handy appliances. Any skilled workman, however little he might know about

[11]   Conclusion of section I:
         Sense of Wonder

In constructing the outline we have attempted to recognize an underlying scheme of order rather than to detect a rigidly symmetrical pattern. A glance at topic B, 2 in the outline would suggest a paragraph or a sequence of three paragraphs in which topics a, b, and c were given more or less equal development; actually discussion of topic c takes up most of the paragraph. The reason is that topics a and b require little development, especially after what has been said in paragraphs 7 and 8, whereas topic c is a matter that cannot be understood without careful explanation. It is not necessary to develop every logically coordinate topic in an outline on the same scale. In this connection look again at the comment on paragraphing on page 117.

Despite a wide range of approach, the selections in Section 4 of this book have in common an awareness of implications beyond the facts themselves. We have seen such an awareness in paragraph 4 of this selection, in which the author discusses the implications of a personal experience. Here, pursuing the connotations of "mystery" in the last sentence of 10, he moves from a specific scientific question to the expression of a personal attitude toward science, nature, and life in general.

What word describes the attitude suggested by "wonder," "reverence," and "humility"?

nature, would quickly conclude from an examination of the working parts of a bee that here was a fellow factory hand who knew the tricks of some highly technical trade. Every hair and joint from head to foot has some special development which makes it an ingenious combination tool without interfering with the proper working of the bee's own person.

[13] The leg of the bee—and I am not here forgetting that there are six of them—has a greater number of joints than has the leg of a human being. Midway between the knee and the joints of the foot there is another articulation, or knee, that is particularly interesting. In each of the three pairs of legs this knee is differently developed so as to furnish the bee with three sorts of very useful tools—pincers, crowbar, and comb.

[14] On the first, or front, pair of legs, there is just below this joint a self-threading needle arrangement so equipped as to make a combination comb and scraper for keeping the antenna clean and in condition. It consists of a deep notch, constituting somewhat more than a half a circle, in the horny shell of the leg, and the open part of this notch is closed, or bridged over, by means of a strong little piece of horny substance opening and closing by means of a hinge. The principle of this contrivance is, as I have said, that of a self-threading needle—though it is more finely and mechanically made than most of man's contrivances. Its object is to allow the bee's antenna to be slipped into the notch when the little bridgelike piece is raised, and then to be held in place, like a thread in the eye of a needle, as the little piece is dropped down and pressed into position. The interior of this notch is furnished with a comb, the fine, long, rounded teeth of which are set close together in a single row all round the half circle.

[12] Observe the difference in structure of the beginning of section I from the beginning of section II. Here the first paragraph is a general introduction covering the major subdivisions A, B, and C, whereas in section I the introduction covered only the first major subdivision, A.

COMPOSITION ASSIGNMENT

Make a topical outline of the second section of the essay. Try scratch versions before writing your final one. The numeral II at the head of your outline should be followed by a phrase which will serve as a title for this portion.

The little horny piece which closes the opening does not carry any teeth, but has a sharpened edge. When the bee's feeler, or antenna, is slipped into the opening and drawn through, the little horny piece presses it down against the teeth.

[15] As a bee's feelers carry its "smell hollows" and the fine, peculiarly designed hairs which serve somehow as a means of communication between bees, it is important that they be kept free from sticky substances and the accumulation of a summer's dust. With these comb-and-scraper devices placed so conveniently on the front legs—one for each antenna to right and left—the bee can slip her feelers into these self-threading inventions alternately and so keep her means of communication in working order with a minimum of time and trouble.

[16] Looking now at the middle pair of legs, and turning our attention to this same joint upon either one of them, we find a very different sort of arrangement. Sprouting out from beneath the hard shell of the leg, at the edge just above the joint, is a process or prong which I can best describe as being a diminutive elephant's tusk. It has the same curve, proportions, and general appearance of utility. This is the bee's combination pick and crowbar; and she uses it particularly for loosening the close-packed pollen in her pollen basket—which she carries upon her hind pair of legs—and pushing it out into the cell in which it is to be stored.

[17] Anyone who has had even a little experience in gardening knows how a packed soil may be loosened with a single tine of a potato fork, or how the worker in the most stubborn soils easily conquers with the point of a pick. For a better illustration, watch the grocer as he separates a pound of dates from the close-packed

[17] Observe the development by analogy—that is, the comparison with tools and processes similar in function. Such analogies are implied, but not developed in the naming of the other leg tools.

(a) *List these implied analogies.*

mass, and observe that it may be pried loose only with a single-pointed instrument which acts as pick and crowbar. Nature had like knowledge of adapting the means to the end, of fitting the tool to the trade, when she equipped the bee with this prong for loosening her load of pollen. Burroughs* says that when a bee has brought a load of pollen to the hive "he advances to the cell in which it is to be deposited and kicks it off as one might his overalls or rubber boots, making one foot help the other." It is not done in quite so loose and easy a manner as this description would imply. The tusklike tool is working to pry the pollen loose, the one on the left leg serving to unload the right, and the right doing a like service for the left. "He," as Mr. Burroughs here uses it, must be a grammatical he. No male bee ever gathered any pollen or honey or did any work around a hive. The drone is strictly a gentleman of leisure.

[18]   This brings us to the hind legs of the bee, the longest, strongest, and most elaborate of the three pairs; and here we confine our attention to the pair of knees which correspond to the ones we have been studying on the other two pairs of legs. The hind legs of the bee differ from the others in the fact that they become much wider and spatulate toward their lower extremities, somewhat like a sailor's trousers when well pressed. Rather they are like oars with broad generous blades. Of the three principal divisions of the leg, the upper one is round like the haft of an oar, and the next two sections are flattened so that each is like a blade or paddle. The joint or knee we are now considering unites these two broad, paddlelike sections of the leg.

The author corrects a famous American naturalist in two details.

(b) *Does either correction serve the purpose of the essay in any way? If not, why not? If so, how?*

---

* *Burroughs:* John Burroughs (1837–1921), American naturalist.

These are hinged together only at one edge, the result being that when this particular knee is bent, it opens a wide, gaping mouth with sharp, serrated edges. This is the bee's combination shears and pincers. With these she seizes and disattaches the flattened wax which extrudes from between the joints of the body, on the abdomen, and furnishes her with building material.

[19] In considering the supplies which the bee in the field is engaged in gathering, no mention was made of wax, because it is a product of the hive. It is manufactured like fat in the bee's body, out of honey which is eaten in large quantities for the purpose. On each side of the abdomen are four wax pockets situated in the joints of the hard-surfaced body; and here the supply of wax may be seen issuing, the flat, light-colored wax appearing somewhat like a letter which a man has tucked up under his waistcoat.

[19] This paragraph provides an opportunity for further consideration of the author's style.

(a) *Would you expect to find the comparison at the end of the paragraph in a biology textbook?*
(b) *Do you think it adds to or detracts from the quality of the essay?*

[20] When there is comb to be built, certain bees will hang themselves up on festoons from the roof of the hive and remain there quiescently while wax forms and pushes its way out from the pockets. It takes about twenty-four hours for a stomachful of honey to be converted into wax, the bee having gorged herself with honey for the purpose. And it is the younger bees, which seem to have the most vigorous digestion and wax-forming ability, that take this specialty upon themselves. The festoons consist of loops like a watch chain, each bee hanging by the claws or hooks on her forelegs to the extended hind legs of the bee above her; and the whole loop is supported by bees that have hold of the ceiling. At first they form chains hanging straight down; and then two chains uniting at the bottom form a loop.

[21] When the appointed time has been fulfilled and the bee feels that her wax is ready for delivery, she separates herself from the others and proceeds to a part of the roof where building is to begin; and now she detaches the wax from her abdomen, macerates it—for which purpose she seems to moisten it with some form of fluid or saliva—and sticks it against the ceiling. Bee after bee comes here and does likewise until a little wall of wax has been built up—a crude blank wall on which the architects have not gone to work. From this it will be seen that the shears and pincers on the hind legs serve a bee to disattach the wax from her own body—not from the body of another bee. Sometimes the floor of the hive will be littered with these wax scales, in which case the worker bees pick them up and carry them to the work, regarding them as so much useful lumber. As the hive is warmed by the bodies of so many busy workers, the wax is rendered pliable and soft, so that it is easily united to the edge of a growing cell and worked into shape by the strong, blunt mandibles of the bee.

[22] The wax shears, as we have seen, are a development of the joint itself; and now, for further interesting developments, we must turn our attention to the broad, paddlelike sections of the leg above and below this particular joint. They are made thus broad in order that there may be room on them for all the devices needed in the reaping and loading of pollen. On the upper one is the pollen basket. It is situated, like a pocket, on the side of the leg away from the bee's body. On the lower one is the pollen-reaping or gathering device; and this is on the side toward the bee's body. The pollen basket is most frequently referred to as being on the bee's "thigh," or on her "hip," but this is far from correct. It is on the tibia, which is the section below the thigh; and the pollen-gather-

ing device is on the section next below that. It is important that these devices be low down on the leg, at a considerable distance from the bee's body, in which position they have free scope and reaching power. A bee loads her left pollen basket with her right leg, and her right one with her left leg; and I dare say anyone will see the difficulty in reaching a hip pocket by means of the opposite shin. Bees that carry their pollen in that position are poetical bees, not the work of a practical mechanic.

[23] The pollen basket, so far as its bottom is concerned, consists of a broad, smooth side of this section called the tibia, its surface being slightly concave. It is fenced round by a row of spines or bristles that serve like the stakes around a wagon bed; and there are longer hairs curving inward and over the top and serving to keep the pollen from falling out. The pollen packs firmly into this place like flour or snow, and being held by the row of stiff spines which fence it in, and the long incurving hairs which clasp it down, there is evident need for the little tusk or crowbar on each of the middle pair of legs. Without this it would be difficult to unload.

[24] On the broad section of the leg next below the one which holds the pollen basket, and, as we have already noted, on the inner side instead of the outer, we find the pollen-gathering and loading device. Arranged across this part of the leg is a series of combs, yellowish brown in color, and looking for all the world like the side combs which women use to hold the hair in place. Each comb has its teeth slightly raised from the surface of the leg, and partially overlapping the next comb below. These combs, by being constantly plied over the bee's breast, serve to gather the grains of pollen which adhere to the feathered hairs on this part of the bee's body and then, then the combs are full, to

[23], [24] You should have observed that the author's usual practice is first to describe each new tool and then to explain its function. In dealing with the tools of the front and middle legs, he uses one paragraph for description and another for exposition of function. However, in paragraphs 12 and 13 he uses a single paragraph for both structure and function. The choice between these two methods depends on the length and complexity of the paragraph that would result from the combination, and on the complexity of the entire passage in which the paragraphs appear.

Considering these points, do you think paragraphs 12 and 13 should be separate or combined?

[24] The author never refers to the device discussed in this paragraph by its technical name, "pecten auricle."

(a) *What indication is this of the author's assumptions about his audience?*
(b) *What other elements of the author's style in the paragraph are consistent with these assumptions?*

transfer it to the pollen basket on the opposite leg. The bee bends the knee and wipes or draws the row of combs across the back of the opposite leg just as a man might draw his shinbone lengthwise across the back of his thigh; the little stakes or spines which surround the pollen basket pass between the teeth of the combs and clean them out, and thus the pollen basket, after many such combfuls, is well packed with pollen, and the bee is ready to go home and unload. The whole device works together with the ingenuity and perfect fitness of a piece of agricultural machinery.

25 The feathered hairs on parts of the body are an indispensable part of the machine. These are hairs which have other little hairs growing all over them, giving them a feathered or mosslike appearance. They serve to entangle and hold the grains of pollen better than ordinary smooth hairs would do. On other parts of the bee's body the hairs are smooth, but these are of different sizes and proportions according to the functions they serve, and are grouped, as we have seen, with various objects in view. On the front pair of legs is an arrangement of hairs which serves the bee as an eye brush. As bees have no eyelids on their compound eyes, and are always thrusting their heads into the flour bins of the summer's blossoms, they would seem to have need of some such convenience.

26 A bee's sting consists of two separate spears or shafts, each with nine barbs. It will be more readily comprehended by viewing it as a single spear which has been accurately split down the middle so that the two halves move smoothly up and down on one another, and the shafts are enclosed in a neat-fitting sheath which holds them together and guides them when thus working. There is a muscle belonging to the sting which gives the spears a pumping motion in the

sheath, first one and then the other, and this muscle is able to keep up the pumping motion to a certain extent even after the sting has become detached from the bee. The consequence is that when the sting is thrust slightly into the flesh the barbs take hold, and the barbs on one spear hold the sting firmly in place while the other spear is thrust deeper, and so on, alternately. The sting works its way in by its own power, and thus goes deeper than the bee could thrust it with her light weight and the limited hold of the little claws and gumlike pads on her feet. Attached to the sting also is the poison sac, which feeds the spears with poison by a groove in their working surfaces.

(Section II of "The Bee's Knees" ends here. In its original form, the essay continues with a section that discusses other special adaptations of the bee and the significance it has for evolution.)

COMPOSITION ASSIGNMENT

Now that you have applied the principles of the topical outline to analyze the structure of a piece of writing, apply them to the composition of an informative essay of your own. This and the following pages give you instructions for planning and writing the essay.

Choose a subject in which you have a strong interest and about which you know more than the average person. The more you can write from personal experience and observation, the more interesting the essay is likely to be. From the beginning of the planning and throughout the writing, you should remember that a good informative essay not only contains an orderly exposition of factual details, but also suggests the meaning or interest the subject has for the writer.

A. First, submit a topical outline for your teacher's consideration. Here an important point must be made: it is unlikely that anyone can succeed in constructing a logical outline by moving straight ahead from the beginning, assigning numbers and letters to topics as they come to mind. If this were possible, one might as well write the essay without preliminary organization. Instead, you should begin by making a rough list of topics and details and then experiment with possible groupings under various heads. An outline that is not the product of considerable experimentation is likely to be more of a hindrance than a help.

B. Second, use your topical outline as the basis of an "expanded outline." This consists of a topical outline expanded by the addition of a sentence outline (see Summary, p. 25) and the inclusion of specific information and illustration. The following outline and commentary illustrates and explains the procedure.

Example of the Expanded Outline

Auto Accidents, A Needless Waste Of Life

INTRODUCTION

While Americans fret about protecting themselves against Armageddon, they remain too lethargic to take action against the unnecessary carnage of the modern highway.

    A. 2500 killed last year; ten times as many injured

    B. Cost of property and compensation of victims

This is the topic sentence of the introductory paragraph. It will be developed by sentences discussing points A and B.

I. Causes

The commonest causes of auto accidents fall into three categories: those attributable to bad roads, those attributable to the vehicle, and those attributable to deficiencies of the driver.

The sentence under the heading "Causes" is a topic sentence for section I. It points to three basic subdivisions, A, B, and C. It might be logical to develop each of these in a single paragraph; but, as noted in the outlining of *The Bee's Knees*, different degrees of complexity may require different paragraphing of logically coordinate sub-sections. Observe the paragraphing of section I, A, B, and C.

    A. Roads

        The least common assignable cause is the road; however, statistics show that roughly fifteen percent of all accidents can be attributed to either poor design or inadequate maintenance of roads.

The sentence under A (Roads) is the topic sentence of the single paragraph that is to develop this sub-section.

1. Design
   a. Blind spots
   b. Distractions
   c. Monotony (e.g., Maine Turnpike)
   d. Level crossings (e.g., U.S. 1 at Saugus)

Still, the best roads are highways to death if not well maintained.

2. Maintenance
   a. Condition of surface
   b. Drainage
   c. Ice and snow

The sentence after 1 (d) is a transitional sentence connecting the two sub-topics of the paragraph devoted to A (Roads).

Note that in 1 (c) and (d) the writer has indicated specific illustrations of dangerous road design.

B. The vehicle

Of still greater importance than the road is the vehicle to which the driver trusts his life.

1. Design
   a. Seating
   b. Steering wheel
   c. Brakes
   d. Glaring headlights

The writer intends to devote two paragraphs to sub-section B.

The first sentence under B is a transitional sentence leading into discussion of the second group of causes of auto accidents.

Instead of driving vehicles designed to get us to our destination as safely as possible, most of us are driving glamorous weapons of mayhem and suicide.

This is a topic sentence which will conclude the first of the two paragraphs on the vehicle.

Even the best of design will not guard against failures attributable to careless maintenance.

2. Mechanical condition
   a. Steering linkage
   b. Brakes
   c. Tires
   d. Muffler

This sentence is the topic sentence beginning the second paragraph on the vehicle. The paragraph will continue with the specific hazards attributable to sub-topics (a) through (d).

C. The driver

Even if all Americans drove totally safe cars on roads which posed no hazards, we would still have more than half the accidents which now occur, for sixty-five percent of all accidents are attributable to the driver.

1. Condition of the driver
   a. Physical

This sentence makes a transition from sub-sections A and B to sub-section C of section I, which consists of an analysis of causes. It also serves as the topic sentence for sub-section C.

i. Heart
ii. Vision
iii. Hearing
b. Psychological (e.g., effect of J. R.'s quarrel with his employer)

Even drivers in good physical and psychological condition can cause accidents.

    2. Deficiencies in training
        a. Ignorance of rules and safe procedures
        b. Untrained reflexes

II. Remedies
    A. Roads
        1. Needed design features (a, b, c, etc.)
        2. Maintenance needs (a, b, c, etc.)
    B. Vehicles
        1. Design
        2. Maintenance
    C. Drivers
        1. Training
        2. Periodic reexamination

III. Recommended action
    A. By individuals (a, b, c, etc.)
    B. By legislatures (a, b, c, etc.)

Conclusion

Instead of worrying about dangers over which they have no control, Americans should fight a menace about which they can do much both individually and as an aroused citizenry.

    A. Responsibility of citizens (in general)
    B. Governmental action (in general)

COMPOSITION ASSIGNMENT (*Continued*)

C. When you have finished an expanded outline, you have done the hardest work required in writing an essay of this sort. The remaining step is, of course, to write the complete essay. The remaining problems

---

Note that 1 (b) suggests an illustration of a psychological cause.

Depending on the length and complexity of the development of C, this sentence may serve as a transitional sentence within a single paragraph devoted to C, or as a transitional sentence introducing the topic of a second paragraph, devoted to C, 2.

From this point on, the text presents only a topical outline of the remainder of the essay. The expanded outline would contain sentences and illustrations equivalent to those included in the outline of Section I.

This is the topic sentence for a brief concluding paragraph.

are the presentation of sub-topics and details in coherent sentences and the choosing of words that will make the unfamiliar clear to the reader. In particular, you must consider whether you will use specialized descriptive terms, as Stewart does in *The Bee's Knees*, or use a combination of both methods.

SUMMARY

The aim of this section has been to help you develop skill in a kind of exposition that will be important in much of your course work and in much of the writing you will do in later life. The ability to convey one's knowledge in a way that is both interesting and informative depends upon clarity of expression and an orderly presentation of the material. The selections represent different ways of conveying special knowledge to the general reader. In undertaking writing of this kind, you should keep in mind two principles which have evidently guided the specialists who wrote them.

First, your choice of words is of crucial importance. Your aim is to communicate rather than to impress. You must determine how much knowledge of the subject and its special terminology you can expect of the readers whom you wish to interest and inform. You must also determine how important a technical term is to a reader's understanding of the subject, and if you decide to use one, you must make its meaning clear. Among the authors included in this section, Gerard evidently felt that an understanding of some technical terms would be helpful to the reader who wishes to understand the functions of the brain, and Russell saw that precise definition of a widely used abstraction is necessary to clear discussion. On the other hand, Kinney did not find zoological terms necessary in discussing the paradoxical behavior of bears. Of even more interest we observe that Stewart concluded that technical terminology would be more of a hindrance than a help to the presentation of his theme, which is the astonishing specialization of the bee's anatomy.

The second principle is the importance of organization. In particular, you should recognize that the topical outline is especially suited to the organization of informative writing, for details can be classified in coordinate groupings subordinate to general headings. If the topical outline is to be a useful tool, you should remember to keep it experimental and fluid rather than to regard it as a rigid framework.

EXPOSITORY WRITING—PERSONAL VIEWS

5 | *Expository Writing—Personal Views*

The previous section contains essays which have as their primary purpose the transfer of information from writer to reader. The essays of this section are also expository; however, in these the writer's personality, as reflected in his particular views and the manner in which those views are expressed, is much more in evidence. The individual point of view is especially important in the last two essays.

PECULIARSOME ABE

Carl Sandburg

This excerpt from Sandburg's *Abraham Lincoln, The Prairie Years* deals with Lincoln's reading as it reflected his character and also as it shaped his thinking. What makes it of interest as an essay is its **style**—choice of words, sentence structure, and methods of paragraph development.

[1] The farm boys in their evening at Jones's store in Gentryville talked about how Abe Lincoln was always reading, digging into books, stretching out flat on his stomach in front of the fireplace studying till midnight and past midnight, picking a piece of charcoal to write on the fire shovel, shaving off what he wrote, and then writing more—till midnight and past midnight. The next thing Abe would be reading books between the plow handles, it seemed to them. And once trying to speak a last word, Dennis Hanks said, "There's suthin' peculiarsome about Abe."

[1] (a) *How do the three sentences of the paragraph combine to form a single thought?* (b) *Describe the structure of the first sentence.*

[2] He wanted to learn, to know, to live, to reach out; he wanted to satisfy hungers and thirsts he couldn't tell about, this big boy of the backwoods. And some of what he wanted so much, so deep down, seemed to be in the books. Maybe in books he would find the answers to dark questions pushing around in the pools of his thoughts and the drifts of his mind. He told Dennis and other people, "The things I want to know are in books; my best friend is the man who'll git me a book I ain't read." And sometimes friends answered, "Well, books ain't as plenty as wildcats in these parts o' Indianny."

[2] (a) *What does this paragraph add to paragraph 1?* (b) *How does it resemble paragraph 1?* (c) *Explain the metaphor of "pools" and "drifts" in sentence 3.*

③ This was one thing meant by Dennis when he said there was "suthin' peculiarsome" about Abe. It seemed that Abe made the books tell him more than they told other people. All the other farm boys had gone to school and read *The Kentucky Preceptor*, but Abe picked out questions from it, such as "Who has the most right to complain, the Indian or the Negro?" and Abe would talk about it, up one way and down the other, while they were in the cornfield pulling fodder for the winter. When Abe got hold of a storybook and read about a boat that came near a magnetic rock, and how the magnets in the rock pulled all the nails out of the boat so it went to pieces and the people in the boat found themselves floundering in water, Abe thought it was funny and told it to other people. After Abe read poetry, especially Bobby Burns's poems, Abe began writing rhymes himself. When Abe sat with a girl, with their bare feet in the creek water, and she spoke of the moon rising, he explained to her it was the earth moving and not the moon—the moon only seemed to rise.

④ John Hanks, who worked in the fields barefooted with Abe, grubbing stumps, plowing, mowing, said: "When Abe and I came back to the house from work, he used to go to the cupboard, snatch a piece of corn bread, sit down, take a book, cock his legs up high as his head, and read. Whenever Abe had a chance in the field while at work, or at the house, he would stop and read." He liked to explain to other people what he was getting from books; explaining an idea to someone else made it clearer to him. The habit was growing on him of reading out loud; words came more real if picked from the silent page of the book and pronounced on the tongue; new balances and values of words stood out if spoken aloud. When

③ (a) *To what does "this" in the first line refer?*
(b) *Is the "peculiarsome" quality in this paragraph the same as in paragraph 1?*
(c) *Since sentence 3, which might seem to be the topic sentence, is not sufficiently broad, write a topic sentence for the paragraph.*

④ This paragraph deals with a third peculiarity of Lincoln.

(a) *What is it?*
(b) *Again, write a topic sentence for the paragraph.*

writing letters for his father or the neighbors, he read the words out loud as they got written. Before writing a letter he asked questions such as: "What do you want to say in the letter? How do you want to say it? Are you sure that's the best way to say it? Or do you think we can fix up a better way to say it?"

5 As he studied his books his lower lip stuck out; Josiah Crawford noticed it was a habit and joked Abe about the "stuck-out lip." This habit too stayed with him.

6 He wrote in his Sum Book or arithmetic that compound division was "When several numbers of Divers Denominations are given to be divided by 1 common divisor," and worked on the exercise in multiplication; "If 1 foot contain 12 inches I demand how many there are in 126 feet." Thus the schoolboy.

6 This is a strange paragraph, especially the last sentence.

What is its purpose in the essay?

7 What he got in the schools didn't satisfy him. He went to three different schools in Indiana, besides two in Kentucky—altogether about four months of school. He learned his A B C, how to spell, read, write. And he had been with the other barefoot boys in butternut jeans learning "manners" under the school teacher, Andrew Crawford, who had them open a door, walk in, and say, "Howdy do?" Yet what he tasted of books in school was only a beginning, only made him hungry and thirsty, shook him with a wanting and a wanting of more and more of what was hidden between the covers of books.

7 This paragraph clearly states the theme of the entire essay, which should be clear to the reader by now.

(a) *What is the theme?*

The paragraph is built on an implied contrast.

(b) *What is being contrasted with what?*

8 He kept on saying, "The things I want to know are in books; my best friend is the man who'll git me a book I ain't read." He said that to Pitcher, the lawyer over at Rockport, nearly twenty miles away, one fall afternoon, when he

8 **(a)** *Why is the quotation "The things . . . my best friend. . . ." repeated?*
(b) *Why is "peculiarsome" repeated?*

The paragraph displays the third peculiarity.

(c) *What is it?*

walked from Pigeon Creek to Rockport and borrowed a book from Pitcher. Then when fodder-pulling time came a few days later, he shucked corn from early daylight till sundown along with his father and Dennis Hanks and John Hanks, but after supper he read the book till midnight, and at noon he hardly knew the taste of his corn bread because he had the book in front of him. It was a hundred little things like these which made Dennis Hanks say there was "suthin' peculiarsome" about Abe.

9 Besides reading the family Bible and figuring his way all through the old arithmetic they had at home, he got hold of *Aesop's Fables, Pilgrim's Progress, Robinson Crusoe,* and Weems'* *The Life of Francis Marion.* The book of fables, written or collected thousands of years ago by the Greek slave, known as Aesop, sank deep in his mind. As he read through the book a second and third time, he had a feeling there were fables all around him, that everything he touched and handled, everything he saw and learned had a fable wrapped in it somewhere. One fable was about a bundle of sticks and a farmer whose sons were quarreling and fighting.

9 **(a)** *In the listing of Lincoln's reading, what work is emphasized?*
(b) *Why is it emphasized?*
(c) *What is the point of the fable about the bundle of sticks?*
(d) *Why did Sandburg choose this fable in particular for his illustration?*

10 There was a fable in two sentences which read, "A coachman, hearing one of the wheels of his coach make a great noise, and perceiving that it was the worst one of the four, asked how it came to take such a liberty. The wheel answered that from the beginning of time, creaking had always been the privilege of the weak." And there were shrewd, brief incidents of foolery such as this: "A waggish, idle fellow

10 *Why is this paragraph separate from paragraph 9?*

---

* *Weems:* Mason Locke Weems (1759–1825), American clergyman and biographer, often referred to as *Parson Weems.* His best-known work is the biography of Washington mentioned in paragraph 12.

in a country town, desirous of playing a trick on the simplicity of his neighbors and at the same time putting a little money in his pocket at their cost, advertised that he would on a certain day show a wheel carriage that should be so contrived as to go without horses. By silly curiosity the rustics were taken in, and each succeeding group who came out from the show were ashamed to confess to their neighbors that they had seen nothing but a wheelbarrow."

⑪ The style of the Bible, of *Aesop's Fables*, the hearts and minds back of those books, were much in his thoughts. His favorite pages in them he read over and over. Behind such proverbs as "Muzzle not the ox that treadeth out the corn," and "He that ruleth his own spirit is greater than he that taketh a city," there was a music of simple wisdom and a mystery of common everyday life that touched deep spots in him, while out of the fables of the ancient Greek slave he came to see that cats, rats, dogs, horses, plows, hammers, fingers, toes, people, all had fables connected with their lives, characters, places. There was, perhaps, an outside for each thing as it stood alone, while inside of it was its fable.

⑪ (a) *What does Sandburg imply is the basis of style?*
(b) *How does the fable illustrate this implied definition?*

⑫ One book came, titled, *The Life of George Washington, with Curious Anecdotes, Equally Honorable to Himself and Exemplary to His Young Countrymen. Embellished with Six Steel Engravings*, by M. L. Weems, formerly Rector of Mt. Vernon Parish. It pictured men of passion and proud ignorance in the government of England driving their country into war on the American colonies. It quoted the far-visioned warning of Chatham to the British parliament, "For God's sake, then, my lords, let the way be instantly opened for reconciliation, I say instantly; or it will be too late forever."

⑫ As the previous three paragraphs form one section, so the following three paragraphs form a second section dealing with Lincoln's reading.

[13] The book told of war, as at Saratoga. "Hoarse as a mastiff of true British breed, Lord Balcarras was heard from rank to rank, loud-animating his troops; while on the other hand, fierce as a hungry Bengal tiger, the impetuous Arnold precipitated heroes on the stubborn foe. Shrill and terrible, from rank to rank resounds the clash of bayonets—frequent and sad the groans of the dying. Pairs on pairs, Britons and Americans, with each his bayonet at his brother's breast, fall forward together faint-shrieking in death, and mingle their smoking blood." Washington, the man, stood out, as when he wrote, "These things so harassed my heart with grief, that I solemnly declared to God, if I know myself, I would gladly offer myself a sacrifice to the butchering enemy, if I could thereby insure the safety of these my poor distressed countrymen."

[13] This paragraph consists almost entirely of quotation.

What point does it make which justifies it as a separate paragraph?

[14] The Weems book reached some deep spots in the boy. He asked himself what it meant that men should march, fight, bleed, go cold and hungry for the sake of what they called "freedom."

[14] *What is the function of this paragraph within the section of which it is a part?*

[15] "Few great men are great in everything," said the book. And there was a cool sap in the passage: "His delight was in that of the manliest sort, which, by stringing the limbs and swelling the muscles, promotes the kindliest flow of blood and spirits. At jumping with a long pole, or heaving heavy weights, for his years he hardly had an equal."

[15] *What is meant by "cool sap"?*

[16] Such book talk was a comfort against the same thing over again, day after day, so many mornings the same kind of water from the same springs, the same fried pork and corn-meal to eat, the same drizzles of rain, spring plowing, summer weeds, fall fodder-pulling, each coming every year, with the same tired feeling at the

[16] (a) *Write a brief sentence which expresses the topic idea.*
(b) *How is the sentence structure of the paragraph appropriate to the topic?*

end of the day, so many days alone in the woods or the fields, or else the same people to talk with, people from whom he had learned all they could teach him. Yet there ran through his head the stories and sayings of other people, the stories and sayings of books, the learning his eyes had caught from books; they were a comfort; they were good to have because they were good by themselves; and they were still better to have because they broke the chill of the lonesome feeling.

17   He was thankful to the writer of Aesop's fables because that writer stood by him and walked with him, an invisible companion, when he pulled fodder or chopped wood. Books lighted lamps in the dark room of his gloomy hours. . . . Well—he would live on; maybe the time would come when he would be free from work for a few weeks, or a few months, with books, and then he would read . . . God, then he would read. . . . Then he would go and get at the proud secrets of his books.

17   This is a strange return to the fables.

Can you justify this return in terms of the organization of the essay?

18   His father—would he be like his father when he grew up? He hoped not. Why should his father knock him off a fence rail when he was asking a neighbor, passing by, a question? Even if it was a smart question, too pert and too quick, it was no way to handle a boy in front of a neighbor. No, he was going to be a man different from his father. The books—his father hated the books. His father talked about "too much eddication"; after readin', writin', 'rithmetic, that was enough, his father said. He, Abe Lincoln, the boy, wanted to know more than his father, Tom Lincoln, wanted to know. Already Abe knew more than his father; he was writing letters for the neighbors; they hunted out the Lincoln farm to get young Abe to find his bottle of ink with blackberry root

18 (a) *What picture of Lincoln's father emerges from this paragraph?*
(b) *What is the purpose of the contrast?*

and copperas in it, and his pen made from a turkey buzzard feather, and write letters. Abe had a suspicion sometimes his father was a little proud to have a boy that could write letters, and tell about things in books, and outrun and out-wrestle and rough-and-tumble any boy or man in Spencer County. Yes, he would be different from his father; he was already so; it couldn't be helped.

COMPOSITION ASSIGNMENT

Sandburg tells us of Lincoln's use of books as escape from a humdrum daily life but makes it clear that they meant much more to Lincoln than mere escape. Referring to specific books in your discussion, tell what reading has meant to you. Be honest; do not merely write something that you think your teacher would like to read.

Various questions have been asked about the sentence structure within some paragraphs.

(c) *How would you characterize the sentence structure throughout the essay?*
(d) *What is a possible reason for Sandburg's using this structure?*

BOOK LEARNING
(July, 1942)

E. B. White

This essay provides an interesting comparison with a part of Belloc's "The Mowing of a Field." White is addressing himself to much the same problem, but he approaches it differently and comes to a different conclusion.

[1] Farmers are interested in science, in modern methods, and in theory, but they are not easily thrown off balance and they maintain a healthy suspicion of book learning and of the shenanigans of biologists, chemists, geneticists, and other late-rising students of farm practice and management. They are, I think, impressed by education, but they have seen too many examples of the helplessness and impracticality of educated persons to be either envious or easily budged from their position.

[2] I was looking at a neighbor's hens with him one time when he said something which expressed the feeling farmers have about colleges and books. He was complaining about the shape of the henhouse, but he wanted me to understand that it was all his own fault it had turned out badly. "I got the plan for it out of a book, fool-fashion," he said. And he gazed around at his surroundings in gentle disgust, with a half-humorous, half-disappointed look, as one might look back at any sort of youthful folly.

[1] This is an admirable introductory paragraph.

(a) *What is the topic idea?*

Diction refers to choice of words. "He played to beat the band" would be on an informal or **colloquial** level of diction. On the other hand, "He played vigorously" would be on a **formal** level.

(b) *On what level of diction is "shenanigans"?*

(c) *What are the possible meanings of "late-rising"?*

[2] (a) *Describe the structure of the paragraph.*

(b) *What is the function of the quotation?*

3 Scientific agriculture, however sound in principle, often seems strangely unrelated to, and unaware of, the vital, gruelling job of making a living by farming. Farmers sense this quality in it as they study their bulletins, just as a poor man senses in a rich man an incomprehension of his own problems. The farmer of today knows, for example, that manure loses some of its value when exposed to the weather; but he also knows how soon the sun goes down on all of us, and if there is a window handy at the cow's stern he pitches the dressing out into the yard and kisses the nitrogen good-by. There is usually not time in one man's lifetime to do different. The farmer knows that early-cut hay is better than hay which has been left standing through the hot dry days of late July. He hasn't worked out the vitamin losses, but he knows just by looking at the grass that some of the good has gone out of it. But he knows also that to make hay he needs settled weather—better weather than you usually get in June.

4 I've always tried to cut my hay reasonably early, but this year I wasn't able to get a team until the middle of July. It turned out to be just as well. June was a miserable month of rains and fog mulls. The people who stuck to their theories and cut their hay in spite of the weather, took a beating. A few extremists, fearful of losing a single vitamin, mowed in June, choosing a day when the sun came out for a few minutes. Their hay lay in the wet fields and rotted day after day, while Rommel took Tobruk and careened eastward toward Alexandria.

5 The weather was unprecedented—weeks of damp and rain and fog. Everybody talked about it. One day during that spell I was holding forth to a practical farmer on the subject of hay.

3 Notice the difference in diction between the parallel phrases "Scientific agriculture" and "making a living by farming."

(a) *What point is made by this contrast in diction?*
(b) *What is the difference in the point of the two examples which develop the paragraph?*
(c) *Comment on the skill of the phrasing of "how soon the sun goes down on all of us."*
(d) *On what level is the diction of "kisses the nitrogen good-by"?*

4 (a) *How does the structure of this paragraph compare with that of 2?*
(b) *On what level is the diction of "took a beating"?*
(c) *What seems to be the point of mentioning the German general Rommel and the desert war of 1942?*

5 This paragraph seems to be a continuation of 4. However, it has a separate function.

(a) *What is its function?*
(b) *What sort of comparison is introduced by "summer flies"?*
(c) *What is its pertinence?*

Full of book learning, I was explaining (rather too glibly) the advantages of cutting hay in June. I described in detail the vitamin loss incurred by letting hay stand in the field after it has matured, and how much greater the feed value was per unit weight in early-cut hay, even though the quantity might be slightly less. The farmer was a quiet man, with big hands for curling round a scythe handle. He listened attentively. My words swirled around his head like summer flies. Finally, when I had exhausted my little store of learning and paused for a moment, he ventured a reply.

"The time to cut hay," he said firmly, "is in hayin' time."

SUMMARY

As has been suggested, style is mainly a matter of diction and sentence structure, which are expressions of the personality of the writer. Consequently, style is an important part of any personal essay. Compare the style of "Book Learning" with that of "Peculiarsome Abe." What similarities and essential differences do you find?

COMPOSITION ASSIGNMENT

Recall an incident you witnessed or an encounter with another person which reveals something of the way people act in a particular situation or react to certain events. Use the incident as an anecdote which will provide the basis for more general comments on some aspect of human nature. Take particular pains with your diction.

ON RUNNING AFTER ONE'S HAT

G. K. Chesterton

⏹1 I feel an almost savage envy on hearing that London has been flooded in my absence, while I am in the mere country. My own Battersea has been, I understand, particularly favored as a meeting of the waters. Battersea was already, as I need hardly say, the most beautiful of human localities. Now that it has the additional splendor of great sheets of water, there must be something quite incomparable in the landscape (or waterscape) of my own romantic town. Battersea must be a vision of Venice. The boat that brought the meat from the butcher's must have shot along those lanes of rippling silver with the strange smoothness of the gondola. The greengrocer who brought cabbages to the corner of the Latchmere Road must have leant upon the oar with the unearthly grace of the gondolier. There is nothing so perfectly poetical as an island; and when a district is flooded it becomes an archipelago.

⏹2 Some consider such romantic views of flood or fire slightly lacking in reality. But really this romantic view of such inconveniences is quite as practical as the other. The true optimist who sees in such things an opportunity for enjoyment is quite logical and much more sensible than the ordinary "Indignant Ratepayer" who sees in

In this example of the personal essay, the author has a particular and individual view of a part of life which he expresses in his own way. Thus style again becomes an important consideration.

⏹1 The paragraph is an introduction quite different from the typical introductory paragraph of the formal expository essay. Instead of opening the essay deductively with a general statement of theme, it presents inductively a particular set of circumstances from which discussion arises.

Notice the tense and mood of the verbs in the last two-thirds of the paragraph.

(a) *What is the connection between the tense and mood of the verbs and the parenthetical "I understand"?*
(b) *Is "favored" the verb you would expect in the second sentence? Explain.*
(c) *What is the contrast between the subject and predicate of the sixth sentence?*
(d) *In your opinion, what is the key word of the paragraph? Why?*

⏹2 This paragraph establishes the theme of the essay by generalizing on the circumstances reported in paragraph 1.

(a) *How is paragraph 2 constructed? Why is it so constructed?*

them an opportunity for grumbling. Real pain, as in the case of being burnt at Smithfield or having a toothache, is a positive thing; it can be supported, but scarcely enjoyed. But, after all, our toothaches are the exception, and as for being burnt at Smithfield, it only happens to us at the very longest intervals. And most of the inconveniences that make men swear or women cry are really sentimental or imaginative inconveniences—things altogether of the mind. For instance, we often hear grown-up people complaining of having to hang about a railway station and wait for a train. Did you ever hear a small boy complain of having to hang about a railway station and wait for a train? No; for to him to be inside a railway station is to be inside a cavern of wonder and a palace of poetical pleasures. Because to him the red light and the green light on the signal are like a new sun and a new moon. Because to him when the wooden arm of the signal falls down suddenly, it is as if a great king had thrown down his staff as a signal and started a shrieking tournament of trains. I myself am of little boys' habit in this matter. They also serve who only stand and wait for the two fifteen. Their meditations may be full of rich and fruitful things. Many of the most purple hours of my life have been passed at Clapham Junction, which is now, I suppose, under water. I have been there in many moods so fixed and mystical that the water might well have come up to my waist before I noticed it particularly. But in the case of all such annoyances, as I have said, everything depends upon the emotional point of view. You can safely apply the test to almost every one of the things that are currently talked of as the typical nuisance of daily life.

(b) *By referring to standard reference works, try to find the source of the allusions "burnt at Smithfield" and "They also serve who only stand and wait." What does Chesterton gain by these allusions?*
(c) *What dictionary meaning of "purple" is supported by the context?*
(d) *What sentence states the theme most clearly?*

3   For instance, there is a current impression that it is unpleasant to have to run after one's

3   This paragraph relates the general idea of paragraph 2 to the

hat. Why should it be unpleasant to the well-ordered and pious mind? Not merely because it is running, and running exhausts one. The same people run much faster in games and sports. The same people run much more eagerly after an uninteresting little leather ball than they will after a nice silk hat. There is an idea that it is humiliating to run after one's hat; and when people say it is humiliating they mean that it is comic. It certainly is comic; but man is a very comic creature, and most of the things he does are comic—eating, for instance. And the most comic things of all are exactly the things that are most worth doing—such as making love. A man running after a hat is not half so ridiculous as a man running after a wife.

4 Now a man could, if he felt rightly in the matter, run after his hat with the manliest ardor and the most sacred joy. He might regard himself as a jolly huntsman pursuing a wild animal, for certainly no animal could be wilder. In fact, I am inclined to believe that hat-hunting on windy days will be the sport of the upper classes in the future. There will be a meet of ladies and gentlemen on some high ground on a gusty morning. They will be told that the professional attendants have started a hat in such-and-such a thicket, or whatever be the technical term. Notice that this employment will in the fullest degree combine sport with humanitarianism. The hunters would feel that they were not inflicting pain. Nay, they would feel that they were inflicting pleasure, rich, almost riotous pleasure, upon the people who were looking on. When last I saw an old gentleman running after his hat in Hyde Park, I told him that a heart so benevolent as his ought to be filled with peace and thanks at the thought of how much unaffected pleasure his every gesture and bodily attitude were at that moment giving to the crowd.

specific topic of the essay reflected in the title.

(a) *What does Chesterton mean by "well-ordered and pious mind"?*
(b) *What is the usual distinction between "comic" and "ridiculous"? Does Chesterton make such a distinction?*

4 (a) *What is Chesterton's attitude toward the usual hunt?*
(b) *How serious is the appeal to humanitarianism? Indeed, how serious is the whole proposition?*
(c) *Can you imagine the reply of the old gentleman in Hyde Park?*

⑤ The same principle can be applied to every other typical domestic worry. A gentleman trying to get a fly out of the milk or a piece of cork out of his glass of wine often imagines himself to be irritated. Let him think for a moment of the patience of anglers sitting by dark pools, and let his soul be immediately irradiated with gratification and repose. Again, I have known some people of very modern views driven by their distress to the use of theological terms to which they attached no doctrinal significance, merely because a drawer was jammed tight and they could not pull it out. A friend of mine was particularly afflicted in this way. Every day his drawer was jammed, and every day in consequence it was something else that rhymes to it. But I pointed out to him that this sense of wrong was really subjective and relative; it rested entirely upon the assumption that the drawer could, should, and would come out easily. "But if," I said, "you picture to yourself that you are pulling against some powerful and oppressive enemy, the struggle will become merely exciting and not exasperating. Imagine that you are tugging up a lifeboat out of the sea. Imagine that you are roping up a fellow creature out of an Alpine crevasse. Imagine even that you are a boy again and engaged in a tug-of-war between French and English." Shortly after saying this I left him; but I have no doubt at all that my words bore the best possible fruit. I have no doubt that every day of his life he hangs on to the handle of that drawer with a flushed face and eyes bright with battle, uttering encouraging shouts to himself, and seeming to hear all round him the roar of an applauding ring.

⑥ So I do not think that it is altogether fanciful or incredible to suppose that even floods in London may be accepted and enjoyed

⑤ Here Chesterton extends the principle of paragraph 4 to other common annoyances.

(a) *Explain the relationship between "the use of theological terms . . . significance" and "jammed . . . something else that rhymes to it."*
(b) *Do you find these twists of language effective?*

The absurdity of Chesterton's supposition at the end of the paragraph is in keeping with the fancy that characterizes the entire essay. See page 51, paragraph 9.

poetically. Nothing beyond inconvenience seems really to have been caused by them; and inconvenience, as I have said, is only one aspect, and that the most unimaginative and accidental aspect of a really romantic situation. An adventure is only an inconvenience rightly considered. An inconvenience is only an adventure wrongly considered. The water that girdled the houses and shops of London must, if anything, have only increased their previous witchery and wonder. For as the Roman Catholic priest in the story said: "Wine is good with everything except water," and on a similar principle, water is good with everything except wine.

COMPOSITION ASSIGNMENT

Everyone has at least one individual idea which can be defended most effectively by fancy, as Chesterton has done in this essay. Following his method, begin your essay with an account of a particular event and develop the idea that arises from it by the use of fancy.

6 Here the author restates his theme, and illustrates it again by returning to the flood with which the essay begins.

(a) *How does he define "adventure" and "inconvenience"?*
(b) *Does the reversal of the last sentence relate to this definition?*
(c) *Does Chesterton feel that his readers should by now agree with his theme?*

THIS EARLY-BIRD NONSENSE

Philip Curtiss

This essay is a combination of argument and satire. (See page 16, Summary.) As argument it defends a position which is contrary to the conventional view. As satire it exaggerates or accentuates those features of the conventional view which the author finds ridiculous and which he thinks can be changed for the better.

[1] For several years and in a rather mystifying manner, I have found myself toying with what might be called a Thoreau complex—a secret desire to build a hut and start life anew in some complete but not too remote wilderness. In my case this was, until recently, somewhat puzzling because I was already living in a spot almost as rural as Walden Pond and, furthermore, I had few of the talents of the naturalist or woodsman. I knew or cared little about the habits of thrushes and suchlike, while my efforts with a frying pan were inept and ludicrous. It was not until I followed the teachings of the newer psychology and probed my soul for its basest motive that, eventually, I found the answer. Then I realized that I longed to abandon all humankind and set up housekeeping in the woods merely in order that I might be able to sleep as late as I liked every morning.

[1] This paragraph is an elaborate leading up to the topic of the essay.

How much of the allusion to Thoreau is understandable in context? Look up the additional information you need to understand the allusion fully.

2   At first sight this also seemed to be without logic, for woodsmen, of all people, are popularly supposed to be up with the dawn, plunging into icy lakes and singing yodels, but, nevertheless, my instincts had argued truly. Experience had taught them that what interfered with a natural, human desire to get one's due rest was not quietude or the lack of it but mere social tradition. Whether I lived in East Thirty-fourth Street or on top of Mount Washington, so long as I had one living companion or one righteous neighbor I should have to contend with the whole crushing weight of public opinion. My own family, to be sure, I might occasionally convince by tremendous and spectacular burst of work late at night; but unless every casual caller, every chance tradesman, every distant cousin of wife's, who might come to our door at nine o'clock in the morning, could invariably find me up and rubbing my hands briskly, I knew that the word would immediately go around, "Poor Mrs. Curtiss! Look at her slaving her fingers to the bone while that lout of a husband lies in bed half the day!"

2 (a) *What is the topic of the paragraph and how is it established?*
(b) *What is the tone of the paragraph?*

3   The result one can easily guess. I continue to get up as early as ever, but I still despise the practice. I am still convinced that all activity before noon is a disgusting and unnecessary imposition on civilized man, and at last I believe that the time has come to say so. The one cry in the world at the moment is "Overproduction." In other words, too many people have been getting up too early and catching too many worms. All right, then. Why not simply keep every office, store, factory, and schoolhouse closed until noon. In two weeks not only would the problem of overproduction be solved but the world would find itself inhabited by the happiest, healthiest, most reasonable population since the invention of the alarm clock.

3   This is the first step in the argument.

How valid is the point about solving the problem of overproduction?

4 The origin of the popular belief that the hours just after daybreak are somehow sacred and much more noble than any other hours of the day is easy to understand. Like many other obsolete creeds, its beginnings were pastoral and agrarian, but, also like many similar beliefs, it has persisted in the popular mind long after every real reason for it has disappeared. The sun rises and ripens the grain, we have always been taught. Therefore we must also rise and get in the harvest. The beasts of the field are astir and mooing with the first rays of dawn. Therefore man must do likewise. "And oh the delights," cry the poets, "of treading the meadows while the dew is still on the grass and the blade of the mower swishes musically through the crystal globules!"

4 This paragraph combines with 5 and 6 to make a unit. Paragraph 4 sets up the proposition and treats it in satirical fashion.

(a) *Point out the elements of satire.*
(b) *How is analogy used here?*

5 As a matter of fact, most of this is today utter nonsense, as must be apparent to anyone who has spent three days on a modern farm. Early peoples were forced to utilize all the daylight hours simply because of slow, primitive methods and the lighting problem. Under modern conditions there is no reason whatever why a successful farm could not be run on the same hours as a nightclub—if one had the whim—and some chicken farmers are already doing it. In actual practice the very early hours are the poorest of the day for most farm work, as the farmers themselves loudly proclaimed when Daylight Saving was forced upon them, and as anyone else can discover by trying to mow a lawn while the grass is still wet. As for the poets, a sunrise is remarkable to most people simply because of its novelty. The average sunrise is a pale, feeble thing compared to the average sunset, and no sunrise over lake or ocean can even approach in majesty the rise of the moon over the same body of water.

5 As is indicated by the opening transitional phrase, this paragraph starts to break down the proposition set up in 4.

(a) *Which elements of the proposition are attacked?*
(b) *How valid is the reasoning of the attack?*

6 Domestic animals stir about and moo shortly after daylight for the same reason that I do, myself—because human tyrants have taught them that they won't get breakfast at any other time. Left to themselves, animals keep no hours at all. They eat when they are hungry and sleep when they please. I have seen horses lying sound asleep in a field long after daylight and heard the same horses munching the grass at midnight. I once knew a crippled farmer who milked his cows at half-past nine every morning without the least harm, and a herd of Holsteins which was fed and milked regularly at noon and midnight would come to the bars at precisely those hours in complete defiance of the poets and moralists. Going closer to the teachings of nature, we find that the hours of the average wild creature are just about those of a boulevardier. The early morning, for example, is the best time to catch fish, not because they are just getting up but because they are just going to bed. As soon as the sage perch and pickerel really understand that the dull, drab morning has begun they stick their noses in the mud and stay there until the lengthening shadows of the afternoon signal that the cocktail hour is close at hand.

6 The paragraph completes the attack on the proposition set up in 4.

(a) *Ask yourself the same questions as in paragraph 5.*
(b) *Does the author offer the analogy as serious argument?*

7 Human beings, on the contrary, having once been caught in a vicious system, cast around to find pious reasons for their own feeble slavery. The favorite one is contained in the familiar saying that, "The brain is clearer and the body is more alert in the early morning." But are they? Medical science has always taught that vitality is at its lowest ebb just before daybreak, and I myself do not believe that either brain or body gets into its true stride until well after noon. To be sure, if you yank a man out of his best hours of rest and im-

7 Paragraphs 7–11 are another unit which follows much the same pattern as the previous unit.

(a) *What is the proposition set up in 7?*
(b) *How is the attack begun?*
(c) *Is there an instance of transparency here? (See page 80.)*

mediately put him on a treadmill, his strength will naturally begin to flag about three o'clock in the afternoon; but that is very far from saying what would have happened if you had let nature take its own course.

[8] Consider, for example, the special professions which are traditionally associated with night work—such as morning journalism or the theater. Can any such *esprit de corps*, such enthusiasm and endurance, such hearty joy in the work for its own sake be found in any of the daylight professions? Where do all the riotous, sparkling stories of newspaper life, the glorious legends of journalism arise? Among the afternoon papers, where the reporters go grudgingly to work at eight in the morning and sneak off at three? They certainly do not. They are invariably found among the morning papers where men and women go to work in the afternoon and willingly stay as late at night as anyone wants them. In the theater a spirited matinée would be impossible, both for actors and audience, if the house were not deliberately darkened to simulate nightfall. Study even a factory when the night shift is working under glaring flood lights and you will find both an elation and a concentration that are totally missing during the daylight.

[8] *How convincing are the examples mentioned in this paragraph?*

[9] The plain fact is that a normal mind grows keener and clearer with each hour that the day advances—unless it has been cruelly driven and abused at those early hours when it should have been slowly finding itself. The same, I sincerely believe, is true of the body. Can you imagine, for instance, a Yale-Harvard football game just after breakfast—or a prize fight at six-thirty A.M.?

[9] **(a)** *How does the difference between the examples of 8 and the examples of 9 account for the use of separate paragraphs?* **(b)** *What is the tone of "cruelly driven and abused"?*

10 Let the reader consider in his own case some occasion on which, with a group of fellow workers, he has gone back to the office to carry some press of work far into the night. Did not the task move with a speed and spirit that were quite amazing? And for once did not the dingy old office seem a friendly, fascinating place? When a man comes home and boasts, "Well, we worked until midnight, but at last we got it!" he believes that what has been accomplished results from the mere brute accumulation of hours. What has actually happened has been that under the cosy concentration of artificial light and the day's natural maturity the minds of those present have at last begun to function and have accomplished in a few hours what had seemed a hopeless puzzle during the dawdling, green periods of the day.

11 When do all the great deliberative bodies of the world meet to settle affairs of international moment? None of them before eleven o'clock and most of them much later. The most successful of them—the British parliament—seldom convenes before tea-time and usually not until evening. Why does the stock exchange open at ten if minds are so much more efficient at seven?

12 Now to all this I can see some early bird listening with a patronizing smile and getting ready to launch his last crushing answer, "But don't you realize that if you get up and get your work done in the early morning, you will have so much more time, later, for whatever you wish—for golf, tennis, tiddlewinks, or your stamp collection?"

13 Yes, I realize it, and that answer displays the weakness of the whole early-bird creed. The daylight demons, the so-called efficiency

10, 11 These short paragraphs contain two more examples of the joys of night work.

How do they affect the organization of the essay?

12 This paragraph sets up a third conventional proposition.

kings, do not get up early because they love work—as they like to pretend—but because they actually hate it. They wish merely to get it over with, like any unpleasant pill, and instead of devoting to it their mature, thoughtful hours, they give it merely their driven, slave-like first moment. The ripe hours of the day, when they should be at their best, they reserve for pure sensual indulgence.

13 **(a)** *How does this paragraph turn the argument of the early birds against them?*
(b) *What sort of activities are called "pure sensual indulgence"?*
(c) *What sort of activities are connoted by the phrase itself?*

14 Contrast with this the truer heroism, the finer courage of the man who lingers in bed until eight, nine, or ten. Whether he likes work or not, he has time to contemplate exactly what faces him, to sift its delights or realize its stark horrors. And, if he is not sure which is which, he turns over in the sheets and gives another half hour to meditation. Thus, when he finally arises, his point of view is that of the mental aristocrat who coolly takes off his coat and dives deliberately into the whirlpool as against the coarse grunt of the man who is merely pushed off the dock. For him there is held out no sop of long luncheon hours and golf after three. In the rapidly mounting hours of the day he knows there can be, in his case, nothing but work, with possibly a little chat late at night with his fellows and equals, and then sleep again. But *what* a sleep!

14 **(a)** *For what purpose is contrast used in this paragraph?*
(b) *In the course of the essay how seriously and how effectively has Curtiss maintained his position?*

COMPOSITION ASSIGNMENT

Attack some conventionally held opinion by presenting your own particular view advanced with the aid of both argument and satire. Suggestions are always telling the truth, daily preparation for classes, value of physical exercise, benefits of the great outdoors.

EXPOSITORY WRITING—DISCUSSION OF BOOKS

6 | *Expository Writing—Discussion of Books*

The student is often called upon to discuss in essay form books which he has read. Such an essay is difficult to write. The difficulty lies in the tendency to go to either of two extremes. One extreme is the factual report which is little more than filling in the blanks of a questionnaire: title, author, publisher, date, number of pages, summary of content, and perhaps a short statement of personal opinion. The other extreme is the personal essay in which the writer takes off in whatever direction the book has suggested to him and ignores the content entirely.

The effective essay lies somewhere between these extremes. In planning his essay, the student should be first concerned with what he considers the essence of the book. He should then present this essence with enough supporting detail from the book to convince his reader. Then he may respond as an individual to what he has analyzed. Thus the ideal essay on reading is a combination of the informative essay and the essay of personal opinion.

Professionally written reviews are likely to exceed the capacities of students in two ways. First, they are often written on the basis of special knowledge of the matter with which the book is concerned. Second, the reviewer has a literary background far more extensive and sophisticated than that of the student writer. Nevertheless, the essays of this section indicate to the student possible ways to proceed in writing about both fiction and nonfiction.

DOWN TO THE SEA

Theodore A. Gill

(Review of *A Night to Remember*, by Walter Lord)

[1] The night was April 14, 1912. What happened then is "remembered" even by those who themselves had not happened by then. The sinking of the *Titanic* has a special awe or awesomeness or awfulness in the American memory. It is hard to say exactly why this is. The magnitude of the tragedy made it memorable—of the 2,207 passengers and crew, only 705 were saved. There is a mythical character about the memory, too: water, ice, the sea did in the proudest product of man's techniques; the unpredictable undid the most confidently predicted; nature scuttled technology. But what keeps us all interested to this day is mostly the great store of legend and story that began when the rescuing *Carpathia* docked in New York and that grows still.

[2] Walter Lord has worked a long time to get to the bottom of all the stories. Here he comes as close as anyone ever will to the real story behind them all. Minute by minute the account builds up, always using the sparest statement of each development, always checking details against each other. The writing is done with restraint, but the terrible drama of this existential situation par excellence comes smashing through all the author's reticence. Some favorite legends are scrapped. No heroism is quite what we've heard. No hysteria was either.

[1] (a) *Explain "those who themselves had not happened by then."*
(b) *Why does the author use the three words, "awe," "awesomeness," and "awfulness"?*
(c) *What meaning of "mythical" do you gain from the context?*
(d) *What are the main divisions of the paragraph?*
(e) *What is the topic of the paragraph?*
(f) *Describe the structure of the paragraph.*

[2] (a) *What is the connection between this paragraph and the first?*
(b) *What is the meaning of "existential" in this context?*
(c) *What is the meaning of "golden-mean gentility"?*
(d) *What tricks of style similar to those pointed out in paragraph 1 (questions a and b) do you find in this paragraph?*
(e) *What is your judgment of the effectiveness of the author's style?*

There is an even keel, golden mean gentility about most of the action which makes the whole event far more remote than 44 years would ordinarily make anything. But the desperation in the context of the action makes it contemporary enough to keep you up as long as it takes to finish the book the night you start it.

SUMMARY

This essay is far more brief than a student essay should be. It does illustrate, however, the virtue of getting at the essence of the book before commenting upon it. Although the first paragraph makes no explicit statement about the book itself, it shows the significance of the event and implies what must be accomplished by a book which is to deal with it adequately. The second paragraph is concerned with how the author achieves his purpose. The analysis of purpose should be more detailed, and the reviewer's reaction should be developed in sufficient detail to require more than one paragraph. The following essays demonstrate some of the ways in which such development can be carried out.

4100 MILES ON A RAFT

James A. Michener

(Review of *Kon-Tiki*, by Thor Heyerdahl)

[1] In 1937, a twenty-three-old Norwegian scientist stood on a lonely beach in the Marquesas and caught the first glimmer of a scientific theory which was to make him world famous. Looking eastward from his mysterious islands he reasoned that 4000 miles across open ocean lay Peru, from which a constant current set westward to Polynesia, and from this meager beginning he began to develop the belief that ancient Peruvians, drifting on huge rafts of balsa logs, could have populated Polynesia. It was no longer necessary to suppose that Asiatics had bucked the inexorable currents all the way from the coasts of Malaysia.

This review shows how the analysis of a book may be well supported by pertinent detail, which was seen to be lacking in the review of *A Night to Remember*. The essay is carefully structured. Michener considers *Kon-Tiki* as an adventure story, as scientific theory, and as literature.

[1](a) *Whose point of view is reflected in the paragraph?*
(b) *Which sentence clearly establishes the point of view?*

[2] Ten years later Heyerdahl and five young companions arrived at Callao, Peru, and built the raft *Kon-Tiki* out of nine huge balsa logs, and on it they drifted 4100 miles across the Pacific, wrecking their raft at last upon a Polynesian reef and proving without question that Peruvians could have settled the magic islands.

[2] Note how briefly the paragraph summarizes the action of the book, which put to the test Heyerdahl's belief outlined in paragraph 1.

[3] The narrative of this odyssey is a thrilling sea story that will be enjoyed by almost any reader. The hero of *Kon-Tiki* is the Pacific Ocean. Its vast, surging waters enchant the reader. Its strange creatures tantalize him. Its perils make him shiver. At dusk the men of *Kon-Tiki* leave their raft to paddle about in a

[3] Here Michener approaches the book as an adventure story. The key word is "odyssey," which is an allusion that has become a common noun.

What are the associations with the word?

small dinghy, but the current relentlessly draws the lumbering raft along, so that only by extraordinary effort can they overtake it.

> " 'Once overboard always overboard' was a lesson that was gradually branded into our consciousness. If we wanted to go with the rest, we must hang on till the *Kon-Tiki* ran her bow against land on the other side."

4   The raftsmen came to know and love the great ocean as few have ever done. They studied the dolphins, swam among the remora sucker fish, and dived beneath the raft to watch the strange fish that drifted along with them. For sport they caught sharks by the tail.

> To get hold of a shark we first had to give it a real tidbit . . .   When it turned to go quietly under again, its tail flickered up above the surface and was easy to grasp.   The shark's skin was just like sandpaper to hold on to, and inside the upper joint of its tail there was an indentation which might have been made solely to allow of a good grip. If we once got a firm grasp there, there was no chance of our grip's not holding. Then we had to give a jerk, before the shark could collect itself, and get as much as possible of the tail pulled in over the logs . . . After a few desperate jerks, during which we had to keep a tight hold of the tail, the surprised shark became quite crestfallen and apathetic . . . and at last completely paralyzed.

5   For 101 days the raftsmen plowed westward through storms and doldrums and starry nights. They came to know every mood of the ocean and wrested away many secrets.   They discovered the furiously ugly snake mackerel, which no white men had ever before seen. They proved that the cuttlefish, by thrusting water through vents, could emerge rocketlike from the sea and glide across the tips of waves. More important, they found that with sievelike

4   *What is the purpose and effect of the lengthy quotation?*

5 (a) *What determines Michener's choice of detail?*
(b) *What is the purpose of this quotation?*

167

nets they could harvest plankton and survive on the myriad microscopic animals that comprise this sea crop.

> "In good plankton waters there are thousands in a glassful . . . Some day in the future, perhaps, men will think of harvesting plankton from the sea to the same extent as now they harvest grain on land. A single grain is of no use, either, but in large quantities it becomes food . . . Plankton tasted like shrimp paste, lobster, or crab. If it was mostly deep-sea ova, it tasted like caviar and now and then like oysters."

6   *Kon-Tiki* stands alone as an account of what an ocean is really like, but it does not prove Heyerdahl's thesis that Polynesia was settled by Peruvians.   In brilliant passages the author marshals his evidence. South Sea coconuts came probably from South America and could have survived such a journey only if carried on some kind of craft. The sweet potato is known to have originated in South America, where it is called *kumara*, yet it is found in Polynesia, where it is also known as *kumara*. Easter Island, probably the most mysterious spot on earth, with statues and runic tablets no one has yet been able to explain, bore ancient names relating it to Peru. The Polynesian god Tiki is the same as the Peruvian god Kon-Tiki.   Monolithic stone images in Polynesia are similar to jungle-hidden monoliths in Peru.   And since Heyerdahl's epic trip, it is known that balsa-logs rafts could have ridden the currents from Peru to Polynesia.

6   Paragraphs 6–9 deal with Heyerdahl's scientific theory. They are examples of argumentative writing. Michener first states Heyerdahl's theory, then attempts to refute it from his own special knowledge, and ends by giving his "own conclusion."

What is the function of the first sentence?

7   Nevertheless, the weight of evidence remains heavily in favor of an Asiatic origin. Linguistically, ethnologically, and culturally the Polynesian appears to be of Asiatic descent. Myths of the race speak of eastward sailings, and one of the most indelibly characteristic features of any Polynesian island is the keeled canoe that can sail against the wind. We know from verbal records that about a thousand years ago Poly-

7   This paragraph begins the argument against Heyerdahl's theory.

nesians ventured along the ocean currents from Tahiti to New Zealand. But they went in canoes, not rafts. The names and dimensions of the canoes are known, as are the names of some of the paddlers. But what is more important, the first canoes then sailed back home smack against the currents. And to cap it all, the navigators left directions for sailing either with or against the wind between Tahiti and New Zealand.

8 As for the two great mysteries of the South Pacific, Easter Island and the sweet potato, Heyerdahl's Peruvian theory does nothing to expedite our deciphering of the runic tablets, possibly the most infuriating block in all archaeology. There can, however, be no reasonable doubt that the kumara was introduced from Peru, but the great Polynesian expert Sir Peter Buck points out that a people which could demonstrably sail from New Zealand to Tahiti could have just as easily sailed from Tahiti to Peru and drifted merrily home with sweet potatoes.

8 This paragraph concludes the argument.

(a) *Which of Heyerdahl's points have been refuted?*
(b) *What additional contrary evidence has been given?*
(c) *What is the tone of "drifted merrily home with sweet potatoes"?*
(d) *How does the tone affect the reader's acceptance of Michener's argument?*
(e) *Is Michener's argument against Heyerdahl's science logically convincing to a reader?*

9 My own conclusion is that Polynesians arrived in these islands from Asia. It is possible that the original inhabitants of Easter Island, whom ancient records describe as having been exterminated by Polynesian invaders about the year 1100, had drifted there from Peru, bringing with them the sweet potato. I am frankly suspicious of some of Heyerdahl's science, as when he says, "There were cases in which an island was named after the star which culminated over it night after night and year after year." That, of course, is an astronomical absurdity, for in Polynesian latitudes a given star would culminate during night hours less than 176 days in any one year.

⑩ A final question remains. Is *Kon-Tiki* a masterpiece of the first order? Is it "as good as Conrad at his best"? No. Such claims are presumptuous. Masterpieces of the sea have invariably dealt with human beings in relationship to nature. The six brave men aboard the *Kon-Tiki* are never portrayed as anything but wooden, one dimensional figurines. There is no growth, no conflict, little awareness, only awkward humor. The fault is understandable and excusable. Thor Heyerdahl is a superb adventurer, not a great writer. Phrases like this appear repeatedly: "Little did those on board realize that a real Inca raft lay close to them." In fact, the first 92 pages of this book and the last 10 are downright dull.

⑪ But Heyerdahl's limitations as a writer are forgotten once the nine balsa logs, held together only by ropes, finally reach the timeless Humboldt Current. The book then becomes a vivid account of sea and raft and great arching sky. More than that, this is a book to make one proud that we still have in the world six young men who would venture upon the ocean on a raft, merely to prove an idea. It is good to know that such courage still exists.

⑩ The book is considered as literature.

Is the judgment persuasively presented?

⑪ (a) *What is the purpose of this paragraph?*
(b) *What is its effect?*

SUMMARY

Although the summary of the book is contained in one short paragraph, Michener gives a good idea of its content as he uses detail to support his reaction. Here, Michener, who knows the Pacific from personal experience, can take exception to Heyerdahl's theory. Even if the student is in a position to argue in this way, his first obligation is still to understand the theory and clarify it for his reader.

THE POETRY OF CIRCUMSTANCE

Kenneth Payson Kempton

(Review of *Captain Horatio Hornblower*, by C. S. Forester)

[1] Merely "the poetry of circumstance," Stevenson once called romance. In a rousing adventure story who cares for character? ("Faria is a thing of packthread and Dantes little more than a name.") All the reader wants, he said, is "fit and striking incident," action "where the interest turns, not . . . on the passionate slips and hesitations of the conscience, but on the problems of the body and of the practical intelligence, in clean open-air adventure, the shock of arms or the diplomacy of life." He was writing of Scott.

[2] Cecil Scott Forester has never been content with this view. His early romances, quick-moving and exciting, outreached Stevenson's dogma in a bold attempt to motivate incident in "fit and striking" character, of whatever historical age. The effect was fresh and the man was cheered—perhaps somewhat skeptically, since he seemed to be reaching for the moon. Two years ago came "Beat to Quarters" and last year, "Ship of the Line": chapters in the stormy life of Captain Horatio Hornblower, R. N. The present volume includes these narratives and with a final section, "Flying Colours," (also published separately in a single volume) brings the study to a close. Looking back on the whole story, on the figure as it shaped itself and on all the events chosen to body it forth, it is possible now to consider how far Forester's defiance will get him.

Unlike the previous review, which deals with three topics successively, this essay is an example of complex development of a single theme.

[1] (a) *Why has Kempton begun the essay by quoting Robert Louis Stevenson?*
(b) *With the aid of the dictionary, determine the relationship between "romance" and "adventure story" in sentences 1 and 2.*
(c) *What does Kempton mean by "passionate slips and hesitations of the conscience"?*

[2] This paragraph introduces the theme of the essay.

(a) *Is the quotation in the previous paragraph "dogma"?*
(b) *How does the comment on Forester's previous work make clear the approach Kempton is to take to* Flying Colors?
(c) *Which sentence introduces the theme?*
(d) *What is the purpose of the last sentence?*

3 The time is that of the Napoleonic Wars. Sealed orders send Hornblower's *Lydia* round the Horn on a venture commercial as well as military, and the resulting battle, half lost and half won, sets the key of the entire story. Home again and penniless, Hornblower is given the *Sutherland* and convoy duty in the Mediterranean; his subsequent raids on Napoleonic Spain are ended by capture. Headed for a Vincennes firing squad with his First Lieutenant Bush and his Coxswain Brown, Hornblower escapes from the coach bearing them across France and in a homemade punt cruises disguised down the Loire to Nantes, retakes a British cutter, and rejoins the fleet—having long since been given up for dead—in a modest triumph.

3 This paragraph briefly summarizes the plot of the novel and indicates its historical setting.

Why does it not come earlier in the essay?

4 That is the outline, frankly episodic and unilateral; and though it is usually interesting and often thrilling, it simply doesn't matter. Almost consistently our interest turns on precisely what Stevenson said it needn't: "the passionate slips and hesitations" of a human spirit. It is Hornblower that matters. His game of whist with midshipmen while lying in wait for a ship of twice his tonnage; his grief over the presentation sword, surrendered to Spaniards, and returned to him stripped of its gold; his boyish delight in a swimming party, with nine naked shellbacks, bent on burning a merchantman; his removal of the ligatures from Bush's wound; the cruise of the punt, the delicate balance between discipline and expediency when our captain, our "hero," proves the worst camper and the feeblest waterman—these inward conflicts are more compelling than any mere "shock of arms" could be, for of course they go deeper. No romantic ethical causality reigns here. No climax distracts with artificial pattern: the great sea-fight comes in the middle

4 This paragraph takes up the theme introduced in paragraph 2 and discusses it in detail.

(a) *What do the terms "episodic" and "unilateral" say about the story?*
(b) *Taken together, the first two sentences make what point about the novel?*
(c) *Using the dictionary, determine what is meant by "romantic ethical causality."*
(d) *How is the final sentence related to paragraph 1? to paragraph 2?*

of "Beat to Quarters," brisk action spreads almost continuously through "Ship of the Line," and in the final section it so happens that the most stirring physical events occur early. But what compels the reader to keep reading, a realistic curve of far greater significance, is the cumulative impact on Hornblower of himself and of other men. And the grand climax is his emergence as a living man.

[5] I said "almost consistently." One phase alone is disappointing. There is sex in the book as by Forester's realistic creed there would have to be. You will recall that Stevenson and Walter Scott for that matter, merely looked the other way. It was the highest hurdle, apparently. Forester clears it, not cleanly or honestly, but looking all elbows and knees, by old style cliche. "A man whom women love easily"?—this painfully shy, angular introvert who covers unease with harsh words and is tempted to giggle in moments of stress? "A man whom women love easily"?—this naval captain who lies with his wife while clammily yearning for another's, who almost perfunctorily seduces a third lady (the daughter-in-law of his French host), and returns home after long absence to find the wife conveniently dead and the mistress (she is Wellington's sister) magically eager? No. Hornblower the lover is neither picaresque rogue nor romantic hero, he is neither sound romance nor convincing reality.

[6] There may be an omen here. Perhaps it is impossible, in this important respect, to do the job that Forester has set out so bravely and so intelligently to do. The fact is, women have no place in this story. Lady Barbara's appearance aboard the *Lydia* is barely plausible, a sop to convention; Hornblower's wavering between her and his Maria through the latter half of the

[5] (a) *What is the connection between Hornblower the lover and the theme of the essay?*
(b) *Explain how the paragraph is constructed.*

[6] (a) *What precisely is the point of this paragraph?*
(b) *What is its part in the development of the essay?*

173

book seems (since he is far from both and unlikely to see either again) more than dragged in;
and the casual affair with the Vicontesse, flatly
unconvincing, was too evidently contrived only
to enliven a dull winter while the punt was being
built. Perhaps Stevenson was nearer right after
all, and this is what he meant by proscribing
"the passionate slips and hesitations of the
conscience." The fact that Romance still
carries generally the flavor of unreal, conventional love that it has held since the Middle
Ages, shows a reader predilection that may be
unconquerable. Perhaps no realist can debunk
that side of historical fiction.

[7] This remains Forester's problem. But at
least one of his heartiest admirers, having an
eye on the very few fables that are great because they achieve the impossible, is knocking
wood.

[7] *What is Kempton's assessment of the
position of the book in literature?*

SUMMARY

This essay is particularly useful in showing the
advantages of concentrating on one feature of a book.
Kempton concentrates upon character because he
finds the characterization of Hornblower essential to
the success of the series. For another book it might be
setting; for another, action; for another, theme.
Kempton is also dealing with literary theory; indeed,
the pursuit of a particular theory is what unifies the
essay.

CHILDREN, PARENTS, AND PIRATES

Granville Hicks

(Review of *A High Wind in Jamaica*, by Richard Hughes)

[1] Although he has also written stories, poems, and plays, Hughes has thus far written only three novels. All of them have great merit, but *High Wind in Jamaica* stands out, for there is nothing quite like it. There is, of course, something a little like it, and that is William Golding's *Lord of the Flies*, which reminded many reviewers of Hughes's much earlier novel. (I wonder whether the success of Golding's book as a movie inspired the filming of *High Wind*.) But, as I discovered in rereading *High Wind*, the books are not much alike after all. Both present children who, under certain circumstances, behave like savages, but the attitudes of the authors toward the phenomena they describe are very different.

[2] Unlike *Lord of the Flies*, which begins with the children already deposited on their uninhabited island, *High Wind* shows us the background of the five Bas-Thorntons. Children of a very British but not very prosperous shopkeeper on Jamaica, they live on an old plantation. Although in most ways they run wild, their mother tries to instill conventional British middle-class notions. In fact, however, they pay little attention to either of their parents, who have not the least idea of what goes on in the children's minds.

[3] After a hurricane, briefly but magnificently described, the Bas-Thorntons decide that the children must be educated in England, and they

This review is an interesting example of the comparison of two works which has as its purpose the evaluation of one of them.

[1] This paragraph, actually the third of the entire review, introduces the comparison of *High Wind in Jamaica* and *Lord of the Flies*.

(a) *In what way are the two books alike?*
(b) *In what way are they different?*
(c) *Look up "phenomena." Which of the two basic meanings is suggested by the context?*

[2] Here a second difference between the two books is stated.

What is the difference? Is it related to the difference mentioned in the first paragraph?

are put on board a sailing ship, which also carries the children of neighbors, Margaret and Harry Fernandez. The ship is intercepted and despoiled by pirates, who, without intending to, make off with the children.

[4] The pirates are ineffectual and in many ways softhearted, but Hughes is careful not to make them ridiculous; these are not characters out of Gilbert and Sullivan. The children adapt themselves easily to their new environment— "They were all by now just as much at home on the schooner as they had been in Jamaica"— and they can ignore what they do not understand. When the oldest of the Bas-Thorntons, John, vanishes, they ask no questions. Emily, the next oldest and the one into whose mind Hughes most often takes us, becomes "far fonder" of the captain and mate "than she had ever been of her parents." After one thing and another, the children become too much for the pirates, who manage to persuade the captain of a steamship to take them to England.

[5] A passenger on the ship seizes one of the smaller children, crying, "The little angel! You poor little man, what horrors you have been through! How will you ever forget them?" The fact is, of course, that the children, with the exception of Emily, are not aware of having been through any horrors, and, in this new environment, their experiences on the pirate ship become a romantic blur. Watching them at play, the sentimental passenger finds it "difficult to imagine that these happy-looking creatures had been, for months together, in hourly danger of their lives!" They are happy-looking because they are happy—even, most of the time, Emily.

[3], [4], [5] These paragraphs summarize *High Wind in Jamaica.*

(a) *Why does Hicks present this summary?*
(b) *What progression of thought justifies the three separate paragraphs?*

[6] Golding, as he has explicitly said, believes that human nature is inherently evil; therefore it is predictable that children will become savages if freed from the restraints of civilization. This is not at all what Hughes is saying in *High Wind*. His belief is that children are not evil but mysterious. Children don't even try to understand adults, and adults cannot understand children. No adult can know what will affect a child's mind or how. Reviewing her eleven years of life, Emily notes as memorable that she has experienced an earthquake and has slept with an alligator, but not that she has killed a man.

[6] Here the distinction between the attitudes of the two authors, Golding and Hughes, is clearly made.

(a) *What is the difference?*
(b) *What evidence does Hicks give of Golding's attitude?*
(c) *What evidence does he give of Hughes's attitude?*
(d) *How do you explain the difference in evidence?*

[7] Hughes's conception of the inscrutability of the child mind is the basis of the irony that permeates the book. The parents, the pirates, and the people on the steamship all make ludicrously false assumptions. Of course Hughes has to convince us that he does understand children, and it is his overwhelming success that gives the novel its power. The irony is often funny, but at the end, when the pirates are put on trial, it turns grim. The failure of understanding can create tragedy as well as comedy.

[7] **(a)** *In what sense is Hicks using the word "irony"?*
(b) *What does the irony which "permeates" High Wind in Jamaica consist of?*

. . . .

[8] Much as I admire William Golding, I think that *A High Wind in Jamaica* may be a more profound novel than *Lord of the Flies*, and this is because of Hughes's ironic attitude. He has no theory of evil; he does not damn human beings, children or adults. He simply confronts, and forces us to confront, the mysteriousness of the human spirit.

[8] **(a)** *Why does Hicks think that* High Wind in Jamaica *may be a more profound novel than* Lord of the Flies?
(b) *Does the word "phenomena" in paragraph 1 now become clearer to you?*

177

SUMMARY

Introducing a comparison with another, somewhat similar work, is often a useful way of illuminating the nature of a book that the student is writing about. He must, however, keep clearly in mind the purpose of the comparison. Note that in this review the emphasis is consistently on *High Wind in Jamaica* and that the comparison with *Lord of the Flies* helps the reviewer to isolate the essential quality of Hughes's book.

ANGUISH TOO HOMESPUN

Henrietta Buckmaster

(Review of *Part of the Truth*, by Granville Hicks)

[1] Granville Hicks has been a literary critic and teacher for over thirty years. He was at one time the center of bitter controversy when he became a member of the Communist Party. As a sensitive intellectual he has encompassed much of the storm and stress, the doubts, questions, and answers that have assailed American intellectuals of his generation. But he has chosen to tell his story in homespun terms rather than with the iron and anguish that went with those years. Something is affirmed by this decision, but more I feel is lost.

This is a good example of a statement of the essential nature of a book followed by a personal judgment of the author's accomplishment. Note that the title reflects both essence and judgment.

[1](a) *What is the function of this paragraph as it relates to the review as a whole?*
(b) *What are the two sections of the paragraph?*
(c) *How are they related?*
(d) *What is the meaning of "iron" in the next to last sentence?*

[2] A New Englander, Mr. Hicks was raised with the simplicity and integrity that obliged a boy of character to make the best of himself. He went to sunday school and was active in the Young People's Christian Union. He went to Harvard. He fell in love with an intelligent and attractive girl and married her.

[2], [3] These two paragraphs list biographical facts.

Why are there two paragraphs instead of one?

[3] He felt so drawn to the ministry—to that identification of God given by Matthew Arnold, "a power not ourselves that makes for righteousness"—that he spent two years at Harvard Theological School. But the institution of church dismayed him, and he was not ordained. University teaching followed, and the stirring social conscience in the best tradition of non-conformist New England.

[4] Few periods in social development can be so pinpointed as the 1930's. They remain a phenomenon. The economic collapse of 1928 was the sharp, violent end of an era. A new kind of stability was needed, a deeper concern for the human condition. On one side totalitarianism was attempting to speak for the ills of mankind. On the other side, democracies were endeavoring to bring about social transformation but were doing so at a pace which brought many liberals to the point of despair. Communism proved to be a tremendous catalyst. Men and women whose concern ran very deep were often "urged to adopt the program of communism while rejecting the Communist Party." Hicks felt that if he accepted the program it was not quite honest to reject the party. The communist slogan was "twentieth-century Americanism" and he joined on that basis.

[4] This paragraph gives some historical background.

(a) *What sentence relates this background* to Part of the Truth?
(b) *How does it do so?*

[5] His account of these years is the best part of his autobiography. The urgencies and challenges of the time required great generosity of spirit and courage from artists, writers, and teachers. There was also much naïveté and confusion, much joining of "the Party" as protest against slowness and apathy, and much refusal to join. Out of all this came, willy-nilly, one powerful disclosure of why the Communist Party never gained the foothold in the United States that it did in Europe—American classlessness. This deep fundamental conviction that each man had the birthright to claim both privileges and obligations was, in a crisis, able to absorb shock and challenge.

[5] (a) *Does this paragraph summarize what Hicks says or what the reviewer thinks?*
(b) *How can you tell?*

[6] The Nazi-Soviet pact in 1939 drove Mr. Hicks out of the Party, though not easily. The moral dilemma for him and many of his friends was acute. From this point on, a sort of obsessive smallness takes over his autobiography.

[6] (a) *What is the key phrase?*
(b) *How is it supported?*

The war years were spent in the little town in New York state where the Hickses had a home. Good-citizen activities in the village, raising a child, writing and reviewing books, paying and receiving visits, eventually teaching again—all are given in cozy detail.

7 But these years of the 1940's and 1950's were as important as the 1930's, and Mr. Hicks was still himself. The war, the aftermath of the war, the new attitudes of the young writers, and the political and social stress of the McCarthy period were a vital part of Mr. Hicks' life. He chooses to deal with these years as though writing for a small-town newspaper. The chatty, folksy quality of the last half of the book strikes me as oddly ingenuous and is certainly no proper substitute for the discernment and critical evaluation that Mr. Hicks could have brought to the books and events of those years. He could have written an immensely valuable book. Why did he do himself an injustice?

7 This paragraph contains the final judgment of the book.

Is the evaluation adequately supported?

SUMMARY

Miss Buckmaster is careful to point out that the essence of *Part of the Truth* is the relationship between Hicks' life and the times in which he lived. An essay on a biography or autobiography should ordinarily concern itself with what the subject represents beyond the mere facts of his or her life.

WHERE THE GRASS IS ALWAYS WET

Hal Lehrman

(Review of *The Marsh Arabs*, by
Wilfred Thesiger)

[1] Wilfred Thesiger's unpressed claim to a rare and double crown is clinched by *The Marsh Arabs*. This strangely withdrawn yet cordial Englishman—part time hunter-explorer and full-time traveller—is hands down the prose laureate of a vanishing Arab world he has made intimately his own. He is also the chief and most trenchant Jeremiah of our times against seductive oilfield wages, half-baked native "education" and urban slums, not to say the electric bulb, automobiles, and other pernicious engines, which, in his view, are conning the nobly primitive Arabs of Thesiger's beloved wastelands out of their pristine grandeur and primeval freedom.

[2] There never was a more apt companion piece than *The Marsh Arabs* to the same author's previous near classic, *Arabian Sands*. In that 1959 work Thesiger—born in Ethiopia, veteran of the Sudan Defense Force, and as much at ease in Kurdistan, the Hindu Kush, Kenya, or the Moroccan Atlas as in Westminster—produced a quiet masterpiece about his five incredible

This review is an example of an apparently uncomplicated analysis of nonfiction. As you read the essay, identify the themes and note how they are related to each other. Also note how turns of phrase suggest, or imply, Lehrman's opinion of Thesiger's views.

[1] (a) *On what level of diction are "clinched," "hands down," "conning . . . out of"?*
(b) *Is there a consistent level of diction throughout the paragraph?*
(c) *Explain the allusion to Jeremiah.*

[2] This paragraph views *The Marsh Arabs* in the perspective of Thesiger's life and previous work.

(a) *What is the combined effect of the comparisons and contrasts of which it is constructed?*

years in driest Arabia: the dread Rub al Khali (the "Empty Quarter") and other man-killing Bedu desert country. Now he reports on seven years in wettest Arabia: that corner of Iraq north and west of the Persian Gulf where the Tigris and the Euphrates mingle to form 6,000 square miles of equally man-killing march, morass, and swamp, in which camels are unknown and the water buffalo is the Arab's best friend.

(b) *"In driest Arabia" and "in wettest Arabia" are echoes of what familiar phrase?*
(c) *What is the effect of these echoes?*

③ Both books reflect a passionate search for "peace of mind" away from the pretenses of civilization, and a love for the unspoiled inhabitants of remote wastes. In a culture of canoes, spears, and huts almost floating on water, Thesiger was enthralled by the chivalry, hospitality, and self-reliance of the marsh people, "the feeling of continuity with the past"; he "envied them a contentment and a mastery of skills, however simple, that I could never hope to attain."

③ **(a)** *How does the first sentence of the paragraph relate to paragraph 2?*
(b) *What is the effect of the phrase "culture of canoes, spears, and huts . . ." in the context of the paragraph?*

④ Again in *The Marsh Arabs* Thesiger vents his familiar wrath over the self shame, bad taste, banality, and misery threatening such idyllic communities through noxious gimmicks borrowed from the West. He finds the efficient despotism of sheikhs over share-cropping fishermen and rice growers preferable to the anarchic stagnation and insecurity of the radio-blaring towns, and he takes satisfaction in a momentary trend of disillusioned natives to return from oilfields and honkeytonks to their swampland home.

④ **(a)** *What kind of choice is suggested by "efficient despotism of shiekhs" and "anarchic stagnation and insecurity of radio-blaring towns"?*
(b) *How does the idea relate to paragraph 1?*

⑤ Some readers may see Thesiger's abhorrence of "progress" and his appetite for physical discomfort as slightly comic. They may even suspect a whiff of flagellantism. Certainly, the perilous diet, the nonexistent sanitation, the odors, heat, cold, and eternal humidities of this

⑤ *Is "whiff of flagellantism" justified by the sentence which follows?*

marsh life, to which Thesiger returned joyfully year after year for visits of months on end, would make nearly all of us blanch.

6 But to each his own, and Thesiger's fortitude is clearly matched by his sensitivity, dedication, and plain courage. He hunts the sharp-tusked wild boar, rides out storms in his frail paddle boat, or mediates blood feuds with dash and competence. At the start this Englishman with his well-oiled rifle and fluent Arabic must have seemed exceedingly weird to his native hosts, but he won wide and true acceptance.

6 (a) *Does the first sentence state the topic of paragraph 6 or of paragraphs 6 and 7 combined?*
(b) *What is the relationship of sentence 2 to sentence 1?*

7 Part of the welcome was due to his talents as amateur physician and surgeon. On each trip hundreds awaited him at every village for free medical attention for anything from headache to circumcision. But mostly it must have been thanks to Thesiger's dignity, his conviction of genuine equality with and full respect for them, which the Arabs could sense.

7 (a) *How does the tone of the paragraph differ from that of 3, 4, and 5?*
(b) *Does the paragraph support the judgment of the first sentence of paragraph 6?*

8 The enchantment of the watery wilderness and its denizens is captured in Thesiger's enchanted text and in his superb original photographs, 110 of them. Thesiger painstakingly describes the Marsh Arabs, socio-political and economic patterns, their fishing and hunting techniques, their practice of bride purchase, the way they build ornamented canoes, and the great Euphrates guest chambers, structures made of reed and matting but cathedrallike in their vaulting and tracery. He seems goaded by a fear that all this "probably within the next twenty years, certainly within the next fifty, will have disappeared forever."

8 *Does the tone of the entire essay suggest that Lehrman shares Thesiger's concern over the disappearance of the Marsh Arabs' culture?*

SUMMARY

In this essay Lehrman suggests his attitude toward Thesiger and his book through the tone he adopts. Where the student writer attempts to follow this example and suggests his own favorable or unfavorable attitude toward a book, he must be careful to give the basis of his attitude, as Lehrman does here.

INDEX TO AUTHORS AND TITLES

Index to Authors and Titles

PAGE REFERENCE TO DEFINED TERMS

Page Reference to Defined Terms

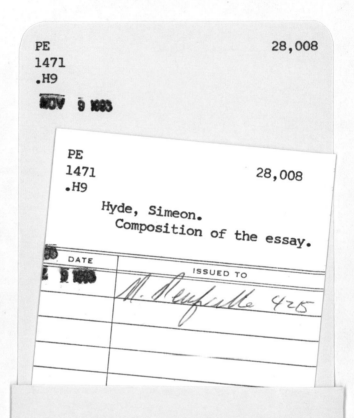